DAYTRIPPER 3
50 Trips In and Around Eastern Ontario

DAYTRIPPER 3

50 Trips In and Around Eastern Ontario

Donna Gibbs Carpenter
Photographs by John de Visser

Stoddart

A BOSTON MILLS PRESS BOOK

APPRECIATION

A large debt of gratitude is due several individuals whose generosity made this book possible. As always, Stephen Carpenter committed himself whole-heartedly to my project, chauffeuring, child-minding and reviewing trips whenever called upon. Norah and Craig Carpenter of Ottawa graciously opened their home to our family during several trips to Ottawa, a critical element in the success of the research. C. William Gibbs and Olive Gibbs provided editorial and spiritual support. Kaitlin and Griffin, with their spirit of adventure, sustained my energy throughout the past two years.

Canadian Cataloguing in Publication Data

Carpenter, Donna May Gibbs, 1954-
  Daytripper 3: 50 trips in and around eastern
Ontario

Includes bibliographical references.
ISBN 1-55046-094-3

1. Ontario — Guidebooks.* I. Title.

FC3095.E37A3 1994   917.13'7044   C94-930282-1
F1059.E37C3 1994

First published in 1994 by
Stoddart Publishing Co. Limited
34 Lesmill Road
Toronto, Canada
M3B 2T6
(416) 445-3333

A BOSTON MILLS PRESS BOOK
The Boston Mills Press
132 Main Street
Erin, Ontario
N0B 1T0

Design by Gillian Stead
Typography by Justified Type Inc., Guelph
Printed in Hong Kong

The publisher gratefully acknowledges the support of the Canada Council,
Ontario Ministry of Culture and Communications, Ontario Arts Council and
Ontario Publishing Centre in the development of writing and publishing in Canada.

FRONT COVER: Mill of Kintail, Almonte.
OVERLEAF: Bellevue House, Kingston.

CONTENTS

Upper Canada Village, Morrisburg.

INTRODUCTION

We are so fortunate to live in Ontario. Adventures of every description lie around each bend in the road. *Daytripper* will open your eyes to places worth discovering, even though they may have existed right under your nose for years.

What is a daytrip? It's an outing lasting anywhere from a few hours to a full day. That means you can have an interesting and invigorating holiday and sleep in your own bed. It also means that the trips described in *Daytripper* are within a convenient distance of home, cottage, work, family and friends. Although the trips in this book are designed to be a day's length, that doesn't mean you can't string several of them together for a full holiday.

This volume of *Daytripper* covers Eastern Ontario, an expansive region stretching along Lake Ontario and the St. Lawrence from Trenton to the Quebec border and north to Algonquin Park and Petawawa. The most diverse region of the province, Eastern Ontario offers the visitor the thrill of a military ceremony or a wild river ride, as well as the serenity of uncrowded hiking trails and authentic ghost towns. From antique hunting in the historic Rideau Valley to the magnificent Barron River canyon to Ottawa's sophisticated museums, Eastern Ontario beckons to every traveller.

The number of trips possible within Eastern Ontario is almost unlimited, but the best 50 have been carefully chosen. *Daytripper* has done the work of selecting the best natural and cultural features the region has to offer, and these are arranged as single-theme excursions. While each trip has a theme, it also includes several activities, so that each day is filled with variety. For example, a trip to a mining community may include mineral museums, rockhounding and a good meal. Each trip description includes recommendations for picnicking spots or restaurants.

Daytripper is suitable for senior citizens, families of all ages and single travellers. While many trips include a good walk or other exercise, this is not a book of rugged activities, and any of the trips can be tailored to the needs of a senior or toddler. These trips have been child tested; well-behaved children are welcome at all the sites mentioned.

Daytripper is not just for locals. It is also aimed at tourists looking for Ontario beyond the major attractions; it can be invaluable for showing off the province to visiting relatives and friends. Take it with you on business trips and to the cottage for things to do off-hours or on a rainy day.

There are a few things that daytrippers will not find in this book. Large, well-known attractions, such as amusement parks, will not be described. They are expensive and incompatible with the local culture and landscape. Most special events and festivals will not be described in *Daytripper*. The trips in this book are suitable over an extended season, not limited to only a week or two in the year. Any (prearranged) factory tours or other special-admission tours included in this book are those that are truly "visitor-friendly," since *Daytripper* adventures are meant to be spontaneous, and don't require a great deal of advance planning.

HOW TO USE THIS BOOK

Keep it handy! You never know when you'll have a day free for an unplanned trip, so be prepared with *Daytripper* by the front door or in the glove compartment of your car.

Make sure you have an up-to-date, good-quality road map. The standard Government of Ontario highway map is very good, and the directions described in *Daytripper* assume that you have a map of at least this detail. Use the trip-finder on the following pages to find trips within a close drive of home or to find trips relating to your particular hobby or interest.

The season and hours of operation for museums and other attractions sometimes change, so if a trip includes a site of special interest to you, avoid disappointment by phoning ahead to check on hours of operation. This is especially good advice for holiday periods. Phone numbers have been provided for those restaurants where reservations are recommended, or where a particular restaurant is a key element in a trip. Please also phone ahead to check on wheel-chair accessibility and other special needs.

Most museums and other attractions charge an admission fee. In almost all cases this charge is very modest, considering the quality of the sites. You won't be disappointed. Some attractions, such as boat cruises, may cost a little more than a museum, but then they do offer a longer outing. The restaurants and inns suggested for daytrippers are average or inexpensive in price, unless otherwise noted. Some of the more costly places may find a place within limited budgets at lunchtime.

Don't use *Daytripper* as the last word on adventuring. Use it as a beginning, and feel free to go off discovering on your own. Ask questions of people you meet—shop owners, waiters and waitresses, and fellow travellers. Ontarians are pleased to tell of the special places within their own area. Follow their suggestions.

Bon voyage!

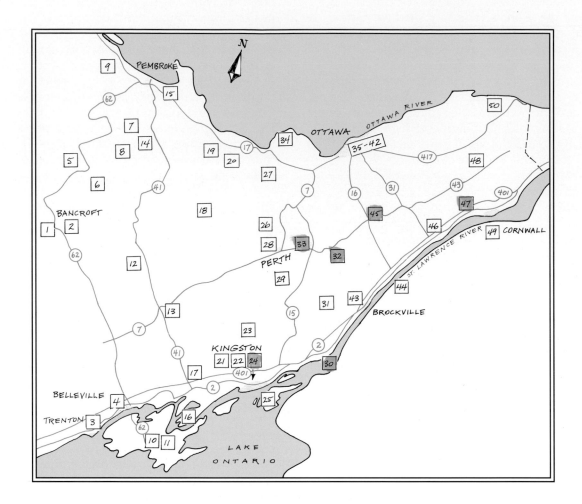

THE TRIP-FINDER

This trip-finder is an index to all 50 daytrips. It can be used in two ways. You can look up a topic of special interest and find the daytrip numbers listed. These numbers correspond to the number in large print at the beginning of each trip description. Or you can look up your home location and find the trips which are within a short distance (approximately 90 minutes) of home.

ACTIVITY TRIPS

HIKING, WALKING
9, 11, 12, 14, 18, 22, 23, 27, 28, 29, 33, 34, 35, 36, 42, 45

FISHING
12, 23, 29, 30, 33, 34, 43

BIKING
10, 11, 15, 16, 17, 18, 22, 25, 30, 32, 33, 41, 44, 45, 47, 50

WINTER SPORTS
2, 9, 12, 18, 23, 27, 50

PLEASURE DRIVING
6, 8, 10, 11, 15, 16, 17, 18, 23, 25, 27, 30, 31, 32, 33, 34, 41, 44, 47, 50

SHOPPING
3, 7, 10, 13, 20, 22, 26, 31, 32, 37, 40, 43

BOATING, CRUISES, BOAT-WATCHING
4, 5, 12, 15, 16, 21, 25, 29, 30, 32, 33, 34, 43, 44, 47, 50

SWIMMING
5, 11, 12, 14, 15, 21, 29, 30, 34, 47, 50

THEME TRIPS

HISTORY
4, 8, 12, 16, 17, 19, 20, 21, 22, 24, 26, 28, 29, 31, 32, 33, 34, 35, 36, 38, 39, 43, 44, 46, 47, 48, 49, 50

NATURE
1, 2, 5, 6, 9, 11, 12, 14, 15, 18, 23, 27, 29, 34, 42, 45

THEATRE
30, 44

INDUSTRY, ENGINEERING
1, 17, 21, 24, 26, 29, 31, 32, 33, 34, 38, 44, 46, 49

CULTURAL HERITAGE
41, 48, 50

FARMING, FARM MARKETS, GARDENS
1, 22, 35, 37, 39, 45, 46

VISUAL ARTS, CRAFTS
6, 7, 10, 13, 16, 20, 26, 32, 40, 49

HISTORIC INNS AND RESTAURANTS
2, 4, 5, 6, 8, 10, 16, 17, 19, 20, 21, 22, 23, 24, 25, 26, 28, 30, 31, 32, 33, 34, 36, 43, 45, 46, 48, 50

TIMELY TRIPS

The following list suggests trips for those times when it can be difficult to find something to do.

WINTER
2, 3, 4, 9, 12, 18, 20, 22, 23, 26, 27, 28, 31, 36, 37, 38, 39, 41, 43, 50

RAINY DAYS
3, 4, 7, 10, 13, 19, 20, 26, 31, 32, 36, 38, 39, 40, 43, 49

TRIPS BY LOCATION

TRENTON/BELLEVILLE
1, 2, 3, 4, 10, 11, 12, 13, 16, 17, 21, 22, 23, 24, 25, 30

BANCROFT
1, 2, 3, 4, 5, 6, 7, 8, 9, 12, 13, 14, 15, 18, 19, 20

OTTAWA
14, 15, 18, 19, 20, 23, 26, 27, 28, 29, 30, 31, 32, 33, 34, 35, 36, 37, 38, 39, 40, 41, 42, 43, 44, 45, 46, 47, 48, 49, 50

KINGSTON
3, 4, 10, 11, 12, 13, 16, 17, 18, 21, 22, 23, 24, 25, 26, 28, 29, 30, 31, 32, 33, 43, 44, 45, 46

PERTH/SMITHS FALLS
8, 12, 13, 14, 16, 17, 18, 19, 20, 21, 22, 23, 24, 25, 26, 27, 28, 29, 30, 31, 32, 33, 34, 35, 36, 37, 38, 39, 40, 41, 42, 43, 44, 45, 46, 47, 48

BROCKVILLE
13, 17, 18, 19, 20, 21, 22, 23, 24, 25, 26, 27, 28, 29, 30, 31, 32, 33, 34, 35, 36, 37, 38, 39, 40, 41, 42, 43, 44, 45, 46, 47, 48, 49

PEMBROKE
1, 2, 5, 6, 7, 8, 9, 12, 14, 15, 18, 19, 20, 26, 27, 34, 35, 36, 37, 38, 39, 40, 41, 42

CORNWALL
30, 31, 32, 33, 35, 36, 37, 38, 39, 40, 41, 42, 43, 44, 45, 46, 47, 48, 49, 50

	LEGEND		
1	Daytrip Number	☆	Start of Walking or Driving Tour
②	Highway		
◄ ◄ ◄	Walking or Driving Tour	┼┼┼	Railway Line

1

BANCROFT
Hard Rock Town

Today's adventure has been a long time in the making. In fact, it began millions of years ago when the rock of the Precambrian shield was created through volcanic activity, intense pressure, folding and glaciation. The result is a landscape of ancient, weathered mountains and a treasure-trove of minerals—over 300 minerals are held in the bedrock of the Bancroft region.

Bancroft's Mineral Museum is located on Station Street west of the York River. The museum displays over 500 specimens gathered locally and from around the world, so it is a great place to sort out your hematite, nepheline, actinolite and other minerals. There are also exhibits dealing with mining since Bancroft was once a centre for uranium, mica, fluorite, graphite, gold and semiprecious stones. Although the mines have closed, the enthusiasm for rockhounding remains and Bancroft hosts an annual "Gemboree" for collectors from around the world. Museum staff conduct mineral-collecting tours several times weekly during the summer; the tours are 4 to 5 hours long.

While visiting the Mineral Museum, wander over to its sister attractions right next door, the Bancroft Historical Museum and the Bancroft Art Gallery. The art gallery features changing exhibits drawn mainly from local artists; jewellery, clothing, toys and pottery are available in the gift shop. The Bancroft Historical Museum is in the log headquarters of the Bronson Lumber Company (1869). Several rooms are arranged to replicate a pioneer-era home, with a parlour, kitchen and bedrooms. Other rooms contain a good collection of minerals, some nineteenth-century English laces and a history of Bancroft's days as a logging town.

Pack your hiking boots along with your sense of adventure and head into those hills of fortune for some real rockhounding. Museum staff suggest you wear pants and a hat (a hard-hat if entering caves), and carry a

hammer, chisel, safety glasses and a field bag. Experts will want to consult museum staff about the best places to seek magnetite, biotite mica, wollastonite and cancrinite and fluorescents such as hackmanite and chondrodite. Novices will want to visit the following sites.

You don't even require wheels to get to the closest rockhounding. Simply walk south 100 metres from the museum along the railway right-of-way to a heap of glittering white stone. Look closely and you will see that the rock is lined and blotched with a lovely deep blue—the rare and much sought-after sodalite. Simply garner your choice of specimen and head back to the car.

The next two sites are out of town, so bring a picnic lunch (if visiting Bancroft on a Saturday, there's a tiny farmers' market near the mineral museum) or head for the Mill Café on Mill Street, one long block south of the museum. The café offers sandwiches, soups and desserts, with a terrific patio view over the falls of the York River.

There are two privately owned mine sites that provide facilities for mineral collectors. The Princess Sodalite Mine is about 3 kilometres east of Bancroft on Highway 28. Once a busy mine, it has mineral collectors for customers now, who prowl in the quarry for a fee. The store has a wide range of specimens for purchase.

Another site, and one guaranteed to please, is the Dwyer Mine. The most scenic approach is to travel north from Bancroft on Highway 62 to Bird's Creek and then head west along South Baptiste Lake Road. This road joins Highway 648 at Highland Grove; take 648 north, which curves west after a bit. The Dwyer Mine is located on Mumford Road, which forms a loop running south off Highway 648. The mine can be reached from either end of Mumford Road, but you will minimize the kilometres spent on gravel if

The daily bounty of rocks for Bancroft-area rockhounds.

you take the *westerly* entrance to Mumford Road (in other words, the second entrance, not the first).

The Dwyer Mine Shop stocks a diverse array of specimens from around the globe—tens of thousands—ranging in size from tiny to gigantic. There are also books, maps, educational kits, finished gemstones and jewellery. You can take advantage of a lifetime of rock-hounding experience, available free of charge from the proprietor, and there is no better place to hear the fascinating history of mining in the region. The enthusiastic atmosphere is contagious, especially for children, who are eager to try their hand with pick and bag at the nearby mine site (equipment rented at very low cost). Kids are also keen about the grab bags of specimens available at a child-sized price.

The mine entrance is sealed off, but the tailings are open for exploration. The mine was a source of flourite, used to make fertilizer, and was last active during the 1940s. Today's miner will easily locate purple flourite, white calcite and black hornblende. Apatite and zircon are also found here.

Rockhounders can ask for directions to the Robertson Mine, which is a source of radioactive minerals (flashlight and rubber boots a necessity).

Whether you come for a day of magnificent northern scenery and a casual look at the hobby of rockhounding, or whether you visit Bancroft as a serious collector, you are sure to strike it rich.

Bancroft Mineral Museum
September to late June:
Daily 9:00-6:00
Late June to September:
Monday-Saturday 9:00-4:00
(613) 332-1513

Bancroft Historical Museum
July-September:
Daily 10:00-5:00
(613) 332-1884

Dwyer Mine Site
April-October:
Daily 9:00-9:00
(705) 448-22372

2

BANCROFT

Winter: Love It or Luge It

Try something different this winter. Instead of griping about the weather and spending a fortune heading south, visit Eastern Ontario and celebrate a magical blend of nature, athletics and fireside tranquility.

The Bancroft area offers a truly unique experience to those seeking exercise and great fun in a natural setting—luging. Although well-established in Europe, this sophisticated form of sledding is relatively new on the North American scene. The Mineral City Luge Club maintains an international-calibre facility suitable for both serious competitors and novices. Drive east from Bancroft along Highway 28 for 6 kilometres; turn right at the sign, and the club is just on the left. You can't miss the driveway that leads up a steep mountain.

The mountain slopes are the foundation for the luge runs. Lying flat on a wooden sled, "sliders" zip down hundreds of metres of track, negotiating sharp curves with rapid reflexes and coordination. Beginners are given a short lesson on steering and braking before heading out. Sleds are turned by a combination of leg pressure on the runners and dragging your arm in the snow. In time, you can work up to subtle shifts of weight and leg pressure needed to steer the surprisingly responsive sleds. Newcomers start out on the final 150 metres of the 500-metre naturabahn, or snow track. With each run, you start higher up the hill, and that increases the speed, numbers of turns (up to 14) and sheer enjoyment. Expert sliders enjoy the kuntzbahn, an 800-metre ice track.

The length of the tracks, the picturesque forest setting and the lack of crowds make this facility the envy of the world. Beware: the fun is addictive! Each run is a new opportunity to handle turns with a little more finesse (and with a little less snow in the face). Luging is completely democratic: the walk up the mountain, sled in tow, leaves expert and novice alike panting and thoroughly warmed up—just the time to take a break and

relish the magnificent view of surrounding hills, clear northern sky and brilliant sunshine.

Bancroft has already produced an Olympian luger, Clay Ives, who grew up with the track in his backyard—literally. The Ives family cordially welcomes one and all to try luging, and they provide low-cost rentals of sleds, helmets and instructions (to those as young as five years of age). There is a snack bar on-site and the Ives offer bed-and-breakfast to those who want to luge away a weekend.

When it is time to enjoy another facet of winter, drive back to Bancroft and head south along Highway 62. Not all Ontario residents migrate for the winter. During the winter months, deer congregate in "yards," locations where there is a dependable supply of browse and shelter. One of the province's largest deer yards, which supports approximately 2,000 deer each year from December to mid-March, is near the hamlet of Millbridge.

Turn west off Highway 62 along the Millbridge road, about 50 kilometres south of Bancroft. Deer tracks crisscross every field around Millbridge, and there are deer in great numbers throughout the village itself. In fact, deer far outnumber people in town, and they wander through front and backyards, along the streets and into swamp and forest. A recommended viewing strategy is to turn north on the main street of the village and then west at the north end of town (at the stop sign). There are two families who feed the deer along the next couple of kilometres of road, and at dawn and dusk, you can be guaranteed the sight of plenty of majestic white-tails.

A perfect ending to a day spent out-of-doors may be found in tiny Queensborough, which is somewhat of a ghost town. Return to Highway 62 southbound and turn east about 3 kilometres south of Eldorado. Continue to travel east, following the bending country road until it becomes County Road 20 and

Luging at the Mineral City Luge Club.

leads to Queensborough. (A detailed road map is a good idea.) The Queensborough Hotel welcomes travellers with flavourful international cuisine, cozy fireside seating and a decor reminiscent of the way the hotel appeared in the 1840s. The menu is eclectic—a dinner may include black bean soup, zucchini salad, pork chops and apple crisp—but it is guaranteed to chase away the chill of winter. Call ahead for reservations.

Rediscover a child's joyful view of winter: holler with delight luging down a mountainside, watch with bated breath as deer pick their way along a frozen river and then find deep relaxation before a wood fire. Those snowbirds don't know what they're missing.

Mineral City Luge Club
(613) 332-4908

Queensborough Hotel
(613) 473-5454

TRENTON
Spend Till the End

Hang on to your hats, shoppers! This whirlwind tour of Trenton and Belleville takes in several factory outlets and bargain-priced stores. It's a day designed to please both the experienced and novice shopper with a wide variety of merchandise and shops.

Vagden Socks and Bata Shoes are among the area's oldest outlets. They are conveniently located beside one another; that way, you can purchase new socks at Vagden and then test-drive them next door at Bata as you try on shoes. Exit the 401 at Glen Miller Road in Trenton and drive one kilometre south on Sidney Street to reach these outlets.

Vagden Socks is a true factory outlet, housed on the second floor of the plant. There are socks for every need, from Reeboks for sporty types to Kodiak socks for inside work boots and Viyella and Bonnie Doon dress socks for men and women in a wide asssortment of fibres, lengths, and colours (including argyle). The prices are terrific. There's even a bargain bin of single socks (10 cents each) for use in craft projects. Vagden also sells knitting wool, kitchen and bath linens, athletic wear and a limited selection of kid's socks and other clothing.

Next door at Bata there's a broad array of foot-wear for the whole family. This is one neat and tidy outlet, organized according to size and season. You'll recognize names such as North Star, Griffin, Weatherguard and Down-unders. Runners, deck shoes, rain boots, winter boots, dress shoes and sandals are available in a wide range of sizes and colours. The prices are one-third to one-half of regular retail.

Reid's Riverside Dairy, Belleville.

The next outlet, Morton-Parker, is a distinct change of pace. So pack up your best manners and head south on Sidney through the centre of town. At Dixon Drive turn west, cross the bridge and head south on Division Street. Turn west on Dundas and then south on Dufferin Avenue. The Morton-Parker factory and outlet store is at number 99 Dufferin. There are great discounts—about two-thirds off retail—on silver-plate and stainless-steel flatware and serving pieces, glass stemware and silver chests. The tea sets are eye-catching and the flatware comes in a variety of styles from traditional to contemporary. The products are first and second quality and there are discontinued lines and samples. The knowledgeable sales staff are happy to discuss their products.

Hop back in the car and head for the 401 east to Highway 62 (Front Street) in Belleville. Turn west onto Bell Boulevard and navigate your way towards the red-and-grey castle tower that identifies Reid's Riverside Dairy. Outside the dairy there's a petting zoo and picnic area. Inside you'll find a slide show, craft shop, grocery store (load up on items for a picnic) and dairy bar (great shakes and cones). Kids enjoy the push-button cow, model train and animated country display. Most interesting of all, there's a window into the production area, so you can watch your milk as it is bagged just moments before purchase. Reid's makes unusual cheeses such as jalapeño jack, quark, smoked Gruyère as well as cheddar, colby and farmer's cheese.

Kitty-corner from Reid's is a small plaza where a tasty surprise awaits. Enter River Valley Chocolates/Domini Chocolates with caution, for once you've spotted the rows of freshly made sweets, there's no turning back empty-handed. Choose from filled chocolates (amaretto praline, for example), chocolate buttons (milk, dark and white), hazelnut bars, truffles and fruit creams. The prices allow for quite a haul of goodies. Displays describe the chocolate-making process and emphasize that the chocolates made here include natural ingredients only.

Bid adieu to the friendly staff at River Valley and head for downtown Belleville on Front Street. When it's time for lunch, the Granary Bakery offers sandwiches and light meals seven days a week in a pleasant atmosphere. Choose from a number of wholesome breads and fillings, although the wise daytripper will want to leave room for the Granary's delectable fruit flans and pies, or perhaps their hollandaise cake or chocolate-filled croissants.

After this welcome opportunity to rest your plastic, get geared up for the last stop of the day, the Samples & Seconds Shoppe. Drive south on Front Street to Dundas Street (Highway 2) and turn east. The shop is 2.5 kilometres along Dundas. Although a small store, Samples & Seconds offers a wide choice of men's and women's clothing, from rugged parkas to golf shirts and from sweat suits to deerskin gloves. Brand names such as John Henry, Hathaway, London Fog, Grenfell and Marshlands cost about one-third to one-half of retail. It's well worth the drive to Samples & Seconds.

Who says that travel has to be expensive? By visiting Trenton and Belleville, daytrippers find that the more they travel, the more they save. Try it, you'll like it.

Vagden Mill Factory Outlet
Monday-Saturday 9:00-5:00
Sunday 12:00-4:00
(613) 392-9391

Bata Factory Outlet Store
Monday-Thursday 9:30-6:00
Friday 9:30-9:00
Saturday 9:30-5:00
(613) 392-0858

Morton-Parker
Monday-Friday 12:00-5:30
(613) 392-9203

Reid's Riverside Dairy
Monday-Wednesday,
Saturday & Sunday 8:00-7:00
Thursday & Friday 8:00-9:30
(613) 967-0449

River Valley/Domini Chocolates
Monday-Thursday 9:00-4:30
Saturday 9:00-5:00
(613) 967-4463

Samples & Seconds
Monday-Saturday 9:30-5:00
Sunday 12:00-5:00
(613) 968-6583

BELLEVILLE
Belle of the Lake

Belleville boasts an enviable combination of attractions that make for great daytripping. The city has a rich sense of history—and beautifully restored buildings to show for it— a popular recreational harbour and several interesting dining spots.

Gain an appreciation for the grandeur that was old Belleville by visiting Glanmore, built in the early 1880s by financier John Philpot Curran Phillips. Glanmore is located at number 257 Bridge Street East; Bridge Street runs east from Highway 62. Directional signs are located throughout the city.

Visitors entering this Italianate–French château home are awe-struck by Glanmore's lavish design and decoration. The Phillips family home was a centre for business and society, and no guest could fail to be impressed by the 4-metre high ceilings decorated with extravagant frescoes, the broad cantilevered stairway and the opulently carved furnishings. Many of these furnishings, including the Wilton carpets, are original to the house. Tourists are free to wander through Glanmore or may take a tour with a knowledgeable staff member.

Glanmore's magnificent dining room includes a gleaming walnut table, a grandiose chandelier and a ceiling-scraping sideboard, and was designed to accommodate 20 comfortably. Another piece of the furniture-maker's art, a sideboard deeply carved with hunting scenes, is found in the billiard room. The ballroom is decorated to period and features an unusual triangular settee (to seat a couple and a chaperon). Throughout the house, oil paintings hang in enormous gilded frames, part of the Couldery art collection.

The second-floor bathroom is a replica of the original, with copper tub, mahogany panelling, silver-plated fixtures and an unusual ceiling sloped to allow the tub to be filled from a tank in the attic. The bedroom is dominated by a canopied bed, covered with a red satin-and-lace spread that is true to the Phillips'

decorating style. Glanmore's basement is home to changing exhibits that examine different aspects of local history, from Belleville's days as a major Great Lakes shipping centre to pioneer life in rural Hastings County. The museum also houses a collection of lighting equipment, considered one of the best in North America. The Susanna Moodie Library and a fine collection of paintings by Manly MacDonald are located on the second floor. Before bidding adieu to Glanmore, you may want to take tea, which is offered in the bright tearoom during summer months.

Glanmore may have been the best in Belleville's days as a centre for merchants and bankers, but there are a score of other homes in the neighbourhood built on a similar scale. Spend a while walking along these pleasantly shaded streets and you'll appreciate what a glory this city must have been in its commercial heyday.

From Glanmore walk east (towards downtown). Each intersection is dignified by at least one mansion, and every side street invites an exploration. Charles Street north of Bridge has numerous well-maintained historic homes, as does Queen Street, which runs parallel to Bridge. Note how many of these homes sport filigree metal cresting along the roof line. The Victorian masterpiece at the corner of William and Bridge, with its stained glass, turret and high gables, speaks of the wealth of its owner, a banker. More modest homes, such as those at 100 and 110 Bridge Street, belonged to merchants and clerks, and were built in the mid-1800s.

Pick up your car at Glanmore and drive into town. Continue with the historic theme by dining in one of two restored limestone buildings. The first is Dinkel's Restaurant at 44 Bridge Street (1870). This block was originally occupied by the post office and the offices of Demorest Bogart, a lumber merchant. Dinkel's carries a diverse menu of seafood and beef. Around the corner on Front Street is the Limestone Café (circa 1832),

The interior of Glanmore château.

which has built a large reputation based on imaginative pâtés and salads, fish prepared with Portuguese flair, and luscious desserts (try the French silk pie). The pleasant patio overlooks the Moira River.

Belleville's City Hall on Front Street is a masterpiece of architectural design, easily the most beautiful civic building in Ontario. The tall steeple with coloured roof-tiles makes it a landmark: at around 60 metres it dominates the downtown and the harbour area. Built in the Gothic Revival style, City Hall was designed by local architect and contractor John Forin. It originally included the farmers' market, which now meets behind the building. Weekdays during the summer there are tours of the interior, which features striking stained-glass murals.

Don't be fooled into thinking that Belleville is a city resting on its magnificent past. From downtown walk or drive to the public harbour at the end of Front Street. How appropriate that a town that started out as a busy port should continue its waterside traditions by turning itself into one of Lake Ontario's liveliest yachting centres. This venue is hopping with action all summer long, especially in mid-July when the Waterfront Festival brings parades, sports contests, art shows and band music. At any season, a pleasant few hours can be spent walking through kilometres of lakefront parks.

Belleville may have been named after the wife of Lieutenant-Governor Gore, but no more suitable name could be found for this lovely city of harbour and mansion.

Glanmore
June-August:
Tuesday-Friday 10:00-4:30
Saturday & Sunday 1:00-4:30
September-May:
Tuesday-Sunday 1:00-4:30
(613) 962-2329

BARRY'S BAY
Rapid Transit

The Madawaska River has its source in the wilderness of Algonquin Park. It tumbles through the highlands of Nipissing, Hastings and Renfrew to meet the Ottawa River at Arnprior. Adventurers come from around the globe to test their skills against Madawaska's rapids, by canoe, kayak and raft.

There's no better way to experience the Madawaska than through the facilities offered by the Madawaska Kanu Centre. From Barry's Bay follow directional signs south along Dunn Street. It's about 15 kilometres to the Kanu Centre, which is located on a stretch of the Madawaska connecting Bark Lake and Kamaniskeg Lake.

The route to the centre is well-worn by the international elite of paddling who come here

each summer to train in a forest setting. The instruction program (Canada's first) was initiated by Olympian Herman Kerckhoff, and continues under the direction of daughter Claudia and son-in-law Dirk Van Wijk. They have added two-hour raft trips to their menu of activities, offering the only white-water experience in Ontario that is suitable for very young children. Reserve a place in the Kanu Centre's Monday to Thursday rain-or-shine excursions.

The camaraderie begins as raft-mates—most groups are an uncommon mix of ages and nationalities—don life jackets. From the centre, it's a short bus ride to the entry point, where all riders help unload and outfit the rafts. Safety ropes are tied around the outsides and through the centre of each vessel, and children are seated in the drier centre seats. Raft guides,

Crooked Slide Park

who do all the paddling, explain a few safety rules, and then you hit the white water. The Madawaska is a relatively benign river at this point, and although rafters get tossed about and wet, you never fear for your life.

At a calm interval of river, rafts are taken to shore and passengers are instructed in safe body-surfing technique (feet up, feet first), and invited to jump in for a try. Starting well upstream of the white water, line up your body with the rapid, and let the current take you along. Only at the rapid itself are you immersed, and then only for an instant. (Now *this* is getting to know a river on a first-name basis.) Then the hard part begins, as you dog-paddle to shore, wet shoes, bulky life preserver and all. Kids and adults alike love this portion of the day, and are disappointed when it is time to move on. If the party of rafters is youngish and in high spirits, the water fights begin, since each float is equipped with buckets and each guide comes with a sense of humour. The guides also take time to explain their trade, advising riders on how to read a rapid, and telling a little local history.

A second opportunity for swimming occurs at a bend in the river, where those who wish may float in a huge natural whirlpool. The water is shallow and probably the warmest you'll encounter that day, so hop out and enjoy Mother Nature's Jacuzzi. The 5 kilometre float ends at a lovely quiet pond, where, if you're lucky, you might see a deer or a family of loons.

The last event of the day at the Madawaska Kanu Centre is drying out. Pick an ideal spot, one of the sunny rock outcrops along the river overlooking the kayak course. You can spend a pleasant couple of hours watching students of the river, from beginners to world champions, negotiate the Madawaska with great concentration and strength.

The Madawaska is not the only white water in the vicinity. From the Kanu Centre, travel south to Highway 62 and then east to Combermere. Visit the Crescent Bakery (cinnamon buns recommended), but refrain from immediate gratification and save the sweets for a roadside snack. At the eastern end of Combermere follow Highway 62 north for a kilometre or two and turn east onto Old Barry's Bay road. It is a short drive to Crooked Slide Park on the west side of the road.

This is an out-of-the-way park, so daytrippers can be all alone, imagining away a century. The centrepiece of the park is the slide, or race, used by lumbermen to move logs around the rapids and waterfall. The abandoned slide is in good condition; its weathered and creaky timbers would form the perfect backdrop for a western movie. The noise of the river, the tumbling swallows overhead and fragrant wildflowers serve to heighten the romantic impact. There are picnic tables, washrooms and change rooms at the park, which is otherwise left in a undeveloped state.

Madawaska's fresh air will stimulate the appetite. There's no doubt about it: head for the Wilno Tavern, advertised as Canada's first Polish tavern. Return to Highway 62 and travel to Barry's Bay; drive east through the hills to Wilno. Mountains of golden perogies (and other specialties) come with enough fried onions and sour cream to sate any hunger. Great prices and service add to the appeal. The decor features a collection of historic photos and artifacts from the tavern's days as a hotel and railroad station.

We all hear enough about Ontario's wild rivers. It's time to experience one of those rivers first-hand, and the wild Madawaska Valley provides a beautiful backdrop.

> Madawaska Kanu Centre
> Mid-June to September:
> Monday-Thursday
> (613) 756-3620
>
> Wilno Tavern
> Open daily
> (613) 756-2029

PALMER RAPIDS
Jack Frost's Paintbrush

Ontarians live amidst a botanical treasure trove. When autumn temperatures turn crisp and trees put on their dazzling display of colour, beauty lovers and botanists alike are drawn from around the globe. Travellers in the know head for Hastings and Renfrew counties for the best colour. Because the leaves may turn any time from mid-September to mid-October, contact the local tourist office for advice regarding the timing of your trip.

This is a circular route that begins and ends in Bancroft. Drive north from town on Highway 62. Look for the sheer granite mountain on the right side of the road. To reach the top, simply follow the road marked Eagle's Nest Park. This is the spot for a top-of-the-world look at Bancroft, the meandering, coffee-coloured York River and the forested lands to the west.

Continue north on Highway 62 to the town of Maynooth (about 30 kilometres). Maynooth's Madawaska Art Shop is well known for its collection of local and international art, and carries pottery, stained and blown glass, paintings, carvings in stone, wood and bone, jewellery and weaving. It is also a good place to find out about the many artists' studios located in the area. Nearby Moondance Antiques is the place for romantic screen doors, antique furniture and reproduction porcelain dolls.

Drive east a couple of kilometres on Highway 62. Maynooth Station is just south of the highway; keep a sharp eye out for the signposted road. Almost a ghost town, Maynooth Station's main features are the McAlpine House, which served as a hotel in the early 1900s, and the abandoned train station and tracks which are picturesquely overgrown with flowers. McAlpine House is now the Laura Lee craft shop, selling decorator fabric and finishing touches such as table linens, china, po pourri and soaps.

Continue east along Highway 62. Between Maynooth and Combermere, the road ascends many-a hill, each one offering a wide-angle view saturated with colours—burgundy (oak), luminous gold (birch and poplar), crimson and flame (maple) and rich greens (pine, spruce and cedar). The lakes glitter in bright sapphire tones, making the whole vista an artist's delight. En route there are signs indicating turns for the studios of skilled artisans; take the time to visit White Duck Pottery, the Highland Tea Room and Wool Shop, and Northernwood Weaving. Be on the alert for Lookout Park Road just east of Purdy; it leads to a spectacular viewpoint high above Kamaniskeg Lake.

Further east, Highway 62 begins the descent into the Madawaska Valley and the village of Combermere. If it is lunchtime, try the historic Hudson House restaurant (see trip 8). Some travellers elect to follow Highway 517 south towards Boulter. The Boulter Road runs along a high ridge affording views of flower-speckled meadows and forest. Follow signs through Fort Stewart (a former wagon stop) and Hermon, where you will turn west on Highway 28 towards Bancroft.

The recommended tour is to travel southeast from Combermere by way of Highway 515. The panorama looking east from the road is amazing. The rolling hills are a mosaic of green, scarlet and yellow; their undulations continue to the horizon. The Madawaska River flows calmly, its legendary wildness apparently stilled by the solitude. Just past the intersection with Highway 514, turn south on Wingle Road to find the Wingle Inn.

Triple-gabled Wingle Inn, made famous in an A. J. Casson painting, is one of the best places to eat in the province. This small establishment serves evening meals to travellers and is a bed-and-breakfast (reservations strongly advised). The food is extraordinarily good, and emphasizes fresh ingredients and Austrian cuisine; the view in every direction is breathtaking, and you'll find the serenity palpable. As the setting sun brightens the

View from Kamaniskeg Lake Lookout near Purdy.

backdrop of mountains and barn roofs gleam silver in the distance, you might wonder if this is a little piece of heaven on earth.

Continue south on Wingle Road to where it meets Highway 514 and turn south; at Highway 28 head westward to Bancroft. For many, the highlight of the day will be Egan's Chute, where the York River surges through a narrow chasm with impressive foam and fury. Where Highway 28 crosses the York River, drive (or walk) along the rough road on the east side of the river. At about one kilometre from the highway, park the car and let the din of the falls lead you to the river's edge. The scene of white falls and whirlpool makes an impressive finale to the day, sure to stay in your mind's eye for some time to come.

Traffic-free roads, superb scenery, haute cuisine and country sunshine add up to a very special day spent in our botanical wonderland.

Wingle Inn
(613) 758-2072

GOLDEN LAKE
Northern Lights

Northern Renfrew County is typically the domain of vacationers in search of spectacular scenery and legendary fishing and hunting. But a few people appreciate that the region bordered by Golden Lake in the east and Barry's Bay in the west is a hot spot for the visual arts. Come and spend a day gallery-hopping where the interior views are as exhilarating as those out of doors.

Golden Lake is the first village on today's tour. The Snowbird gift shop has been serving the tourist market for over two decades. There are crafts galore—many with a regional flair—lamp shades adorned with pressed flowers, wildlife prints and posters, Inuit sculpture, glass miniatures, jewellery, and decorative and functional pottery. The Snowbird's book shelves are stocked with selections hard to find elsewhere, with an emphasis on native and northern stories, Canadian history and quality children's books.

Continue your art tour by driving southwest down the Reserve Road (the Snowbird is at the intersection of Highway 60 and Reserve Road) to Manido Chiman, the Algonquin Heritage Centre. This is a gallery and store with a difference, for guests come away more knowledgeable about aboriginal life and art. The fine display of deerskin clothing includes beaded moccasins and boots, mittens, skirts and vests. There are shawls and throws of parachute silk, bark baskets and antler sculpture. Prints and paintings reflect a special combination of themes, as traditional myths are displayed using contemporary painting styles. Much of the merchandise, such as tamarack decoys, prayer wheels, moose calls, medicine hoops and no-face dolls come with explanatory notes describing use, manufacture and materials. The centre includes a small museum with displays on the traditional construction of birchbark canoes manufactured by members of the Golden Lake First Nation.

A second store on the reserve is Anishinabe Ceramics & Crafts, situated on the same side road as the Heritage Centre. Owner Linda Sarozin offers lovely jackets and vests made from deerskin tanned on the premises. (Visitors are welcome to observe the processing of hides using traditional methods—telephone for information.) There are ceramic pieces with a native theme as well as medicine wheels, dream catchers and sweet-grass braids. All materials come with information on their cultural significance.

Continue west along Reserve Road (also known locally as the Ruby-Reserve Road). Midway between Golden Lake and Killaloe is the Country Crafts store. "Something for every occasion" is the theme, and you'll find that easy to believe when perusing the colourful and diverse array of decorator accents. Huge mock dolls, of mice in calico dresses or floppy-eared bunnies, are a shop specialty, as are hand-dipped scented candles, hand-turned wooden bowls, stained-glass suncatchers, wreaths for every season, pillows, jewellery and pottery.

Return to Golden Lake and head west on Highway 60. The smart daytripper will want to bring a picnic lunch for enjoying at any of the several pull-offs along the shore of Golden Lake. The water sparkles in any weather, the air is scented with pine, and it is hard to imagine a nicer place to lunch. A second opportunity to appreciate a fine view lies ahead, just east of Wilno. Follow signs to the Shrine Hill Lookout. The landscape below looks like a tufted green carpet that has been folded into ridges and mountains; sunshine glints off silvery barns tucked away in the wilderness. Wilno was settled by Polish immigrants who arrived in the mid-nineteenth century. Their sense of community remains strong to this day, symbolized by nearby Our Lady Queen of Poland Church.

Head westward again along Highway 60 to Wilno's original general store, now the home of the Wilno Craft Gallery. In one magical location are the dazzling works of over four

The Wilno Craft Gallery

dozen local artists, the whole effect like a gigantic visual potluck supper, each talented artist contributing something unique. The woodworkers bring turned bowls, intricate inlaid boxes, carvings and decoys. Sculptors add works in stone, clay, wood and bone. Fabric artists contribute weavings, quilts, collages and painted silks. Painters furnish acrylics and watercolours. And in addition, are the artisans working with glass (stained, blown and fused), leather and fur. Much of the art draws on the local landscape and society for its inspiration, and the shop, which mixes a touch of whimsy and a flair for excellence, overflows with the colours of the north. All in all, the Wilno Craft Gallery is one of the treasures of the Ottawa Valley.

Now it is on to Barry's Bay. On the main street of town is Grumblin' Granny's—you can't miss this shop so full of merchandise that it spills out the front door, over the porch and out onto the sidewalk. The theme at Granny's is southwestern and Latin: there are more sandals, baskets and leather furniture here than in the rest of the valley put together.

If you have left lunch until now, Barry's Bay has several good restaurants to choose from. Otherwise, wedge yourself (carefully but proudly) in among your new paintings, moccasins, carvings and candles, and enjoy the splendid valley scenery en route home.

Most shops open standard
business hours

8

FOYMOUNT
Ghost Busters

The Ottawa Valley is a Mecca for those who love investigating ghost towns—those relics of boom-and-bust cycles in mining and forestry, with their ruggedly weathered mills, churches, hotels and homes. Some of the settlements survive in remarkable condition and are situated in the wildly beautiful mountain country between Renfrew and Barry's Bay. (Equip yourself with a full tank of gas and a road map.)

Begin the day at Dacre, about 30 kilometres west of Renfrew on Highway 132. Travel 2 kilometres north from Dacre on Highway 513 to reach Balaclava, which began life as a mill village on Constant Creek. During its mid-nineteenth century prosperity, Balaclava was comprised of a hotel, store, smithy and

several houses. As the local timber supply diminished, the mill's production slowed and finally halted in the 1960s. The visitor of today can see all the original buildings, each worn and warped by the elements, but together constituting an evocative frontier museum. The motionless mill pond, lily pads and stalking herons beckon to photographers.

Return to Dacre and head west along Highway 132. It is 3 kilometres to a northward turn onto Highway 41 and another couple of kilometres to the infamous Opeongo settlement road, where you will turn west. During the 1850s, the Opeongo was one of several roads built into the wilderness to encourage settlement and agriculture. Although several hundred people

Balaclava on Constant Creek.

attempted homesteading along the Opeongo, most eventually left, heartsick over poor soils, intense isolation and poverty.

The Opeongo Road is a terrific drive as it swoops and swerves along the base of the Black Donald Mountains. All along the road are reminders of the last century: log barns sit cushioned by fields of wildflowers, and split-rail fences and overgrown trails lead up the hillsides. Settlers imported a British style of farmstead, with log barns and outbuildings forming a tight square around a protected yard, and this unusual pattern is preserved along the Opeongo.

The road grinds up to the top of the mountains and the visitor is rewarded by glorious views that extend all the way to the Ottawa River and Quebec's Gatineau Mountains. The Opeongo reaches a T-intersection at Highway 512. Turn left to visit the surprise of the day—Foymount—a ghost town of the late twentieth century. This village was an Armed Forces radar base and the abandoned warehouses, apartment buildings, recreation hall, library and school reflect the military base style of the 1950s.

How eerie it is to see such a contemporary village lying abandoned. But history is not finished with Foymount. It appears to be undergoing a renaissance—Sierra Designs outerwear (Black Water Clothing) is manufactured in some of the military warehouses, and several of the houses are occupied. (The factory has an outlet store open on weekends, and sells a line of handsome and durable parkas and other outdoor gear.)

Continue the journey by driving west on Highway 512 to Brudenell. Brudenell was a lively crossroads village of a couple of hundred people at the intersection of the Opeongo and the Peterson Colonization Road from Muskoka. As settlement declined, so did the need for stores and stagecoach stops, so tiny Brudenell was abandoned. A large gingerbreaded house still stands, as does a store and a hotel with a grand porch. As with most ghost towns, commercial structures are now used for residences or are abandoned.

Upon leaving Brudenell do not drive north on Highway 512, but rather turn west on the road towards Rockingham; it's about 6 kilometres from Brudenell to the hamlet nestled in a glen. In its heyday Rockingham boasted two mills, stores, taverns, and hotels. Many of these buildings exist to this day, looking much as they did a century and a half ago.

The focal point of Rockingham, and perhaps the highlight of the entire day, is St. Leonard's Anglican church. Board-and-batten churches are uncommon in Ontario, and St. Leonard's, which dates to 1864, is particularly pretty, sitting atop a grassy hill, surrounded by woods and protected by an ancient wrought-iron fence decorated with maple leaves. The church, which no longer holds services, is equally appealing inside—the Gothic windows frame a peaceful view of the chipmunks patrolling the cemetery, and the tiny village beyond. The guest book contains the thoughts of visitors from around the nation, most of whom plea for leaving charming St. Leonard's just the way it is—and you will surely agree.

The last stop of the day is in Combermere, so travel southwest along the Rockingham road. The Hudson House Restaurant has a ghostly past of its own. This was the home of Captain Hudson, who lost his life when the steamboat *Mayflower* sank on Kamaniskeg Lake in November 1912. Any local can relate the interesting account of the tragedy, and will tell you that on a bright, calm day, the remains of the *Mayflower* can be seen from the surface of the lake. At lunchtime there are burgers, sandwiches and homemade soups and at dinner, roasts and schnitzel. The menu is simple but well prepared, and the service country-friendly.

Venture out on the historic Opeongo Road and you will return with visions of wide horizons, creaking mill wheels and remote woodsy chapels. No better way to celebrate Ontario's living heritage.

Hudson House Restaurant
Reservations preferred
Closed Monday & Tuesday
during the winter
(613) 756-2326

PETAWAWA
Take a Walk on the Wild Side

The Ottawa Valley is a territory of forest, river and mountain of unforgettable raw beauty, unsurpassed anywhere in Ontario. These wild lands beckon to the adventurer of today just as surely as they called to the voyageur and lumber baron of yesteryear. Two sites near Petawawa—largely unnoticed by most of the tourist traffic—enable us to reach the very heart of the valley.

Drive west from Petawawa on Highway 17. Petawawa sits atop an unusual "eco-zone," or natural landscape area. An extensive sand plain north and west of town marks the location of an ancient delta. About 11,000 years ago this land was covered by water, when glacial Lake Algonquin covered what is now Lake Huron and Lake Nipissing and drained to the Atlantic in this very vicinity. Travellers will notice how the jack pine and blueberry covered plains contrast with the rolling and rocky contours of the rest of the region.

This forest is continually changing, weathering the effects of fire and logging and budworm infestations. Find out more about these and other forestry concerns at the Petawawa Research Forest; the turnoff is well marked, about 20 kilometres west of Petawawa. This is Canada's oldest forestry research centre; the first experimental tree plots date to 1918. The centre covers 100 square kilometres, which leaves plenty of space for experimental plantations as well as recreation: fishing, hunting, canoeing (canoeists travel the Chalk River to Corry Lake), cross-country skiing (60 kilometres of trails for all skill levels), birdwatching (180 species) and painting. Most visitors elect to wander the extensive trail system which runs through mature forest of pine, aspen, oak and birch.

Inside the visitor centre are displays on forest management methods, logging, stereoscopic (3-D) aerial photographs, and an educational and entertaining computer game in which players apply limited funds to meet various forest management objectives, deciding

whether to invest in fertilizer or seedlings and how to cope with natural disasters. The centre is also the spot to pick up brochures on two interpretive trails (dealing with the forest environment and forestry methods) and a 40-minute audio cassette which you can play in your car as you take a driving tour of the forest.

The daytripper would be well advised to bring a picnic lunch and enjoy it at the forest station. Otherwise, there are a few eating spots in Petawawa. After lunch it is time for the climactic stop of the day—the incomparable Barron River Canyon.

Drive east of the forestry station on Highway 17 to County Road 26. Turn south; just off 17 is the intersection of County Roads 26 and 28. Turn west on Road 28, also called Achray (pronounced Ackray) Road. Drive 26 kilometres to the Algonquin Provincial Park gate, and then 11 kilometres past the gate to signs (and parking lot) that mark the Barron River Canyon hiking trail.

The 1.5-kilometre trail is a loop that leads to the north rim of the canyon and a view too immense for words. Grey walls plunge precipitously 100 metres from the skyline into the wide brown river. The enchantment of the view is heightened by fragrant air and a silence broken only by the wind's whistle and a woodpecker drumming. The Barron River Canyon is a wonderful place to be alone, and you don't have to travel days to get there.

Naturalists looking for more information on the geologic history of the river and canyon will want to consult the interpretive brochure available at the trail entrance. Anyone will be intrigued to learn about some of the canyon's more interesting inhabitants, many of whom can be observed from the cliff's edge. Lime-loving plants such as a lichen called Xanthoria (the bright orange patches on the cliffs) and Encrusted Saxifrage survive here

Barron River Canyon, Algonquin Provincial Park.

because of the calcium that seeps into the canyon via cracks in the earth's surface. Cliff-dwelling birds such as red-tailed hawks, ravens, barn swallows and phoebes put on a daily acrobatics show over the river. A wintertime visit is especially recommended for wildlife-lovers, because deer and wolves, bald and golden eagles make the icy canyon their winter retreat.

Although the water far below appears quiet, the river was once as fast and ferocious as mighty Niagara, when the water of the glacial Great Lakes drained past this point. And during the nineteenth century, the gorge echoed with the sounds of lumbermen and pine logs filled the river as they were transported downstream. (Some of these logs have remained in the river to this day.)

Energetic types will want to explore more of Algonquin's wilderness. Canoeists can return to a trail 3 kilometres inside the park gate, where a sign indicates canoe access to the river. There is a single portage between the highway and the river. Hikers will want to travel further along the Achray Road to meet up with the lengthy Achray trail system, which has many scenic overlooks of its own.

There may be nothing more deeply restorative than a walk in the forest, and there are few places more easily accessible and more beautifully rewarding for such a walk than the Petawawa Forest Station and the Barron River Canyon.

Petawawa Forest Visitor Centre
June-September:
Daily 9:00-9:00
Trails open year-round
(613) 589-2880

Barron River Canyon
Open year-round

BLOOMFIELD
Artscapade

The scenic appeal of Prince Edward County has made it popular with naturalists, photographers and painters. It has also spawned a thriving "home-grown" visual arts community, and you can spend a happy day visiting the studios and galleries of Quinte's Isle, discovering many high-quality works and meeting their originators.

This tour begins in the northwest corner of the county; be sure to consult a detailed road map. Travel south from the 401 or Highway 2 on Highway 33. At Carrying Place, drive west along County Road 64 to the Weller House of Canadian Art. The gallery is in the historic red-brick home of early settler Asa Weller, and is a fine showcase for local painters and sculptors. Whether the subject matter is local or distant, the work is always refreshingly different and displayed with care.

Drive east from the Weller House, and cross Highway 33 to continue eastward along County Road 3, which has coastal views. Drive south on Highway 62 to the Barber Nurseries. Tantramar, the gallery of Linda Barber, is on the grounds of the nurseries. Barber specializes in watercolours of local scenes and historic buildings. Some of these renderings are in the form of charming miniatures.

From Tantramar travel south to Bloomfield and delightful main street of antique and craft shops. For the art-tripper, there's Tom Mathews's Village Art Gallery—he specializes in local subjects in an impressionist style. The gallery, which shares space in the artist's home, also sells handmade glass lamps. The carriage house at Bloomfield Pottery offers items to beautify any decor, with colour-coordinated porcelain tableware, serving dishes, lamps and fabric. Connoisseurs will want to tour Loyalist Antiques, with its inspiring collection of eighteenth- and nineteenth-century Canadian landscape paintings, including the work of Macdonald and Caron.

Bloomfield is also the home of the Quinte Educational Museum. In addition to a history of the county's school system, there are also intriguing descriptions of teaching conditions and methods over the last century. Kids love to try the quill pens and delight at the rules for teachers and students. ("Men teachers may take one evening each week for courting purposes, or two evenings a week if they go to Church regularly.")

For lunch, Bloomfield has a wonderful restaurant, Angeline's, featuring fine French cuisine prepared and served with justifiable pride. Choose items such as shrimp salad with lime-maple vinaigrette, organic chicken with pesto or Waupoos Island rack of lamb.

From Bloomfield travel east on Highway 33 to Picton, where the art tour continues on Main Street. The Mad Dog Gallery is the best place for an overview of work from local sculptors, painters, potters and fabric artists. It's an impressive display of talent for one tiny island, and the prices will ensure that visitors make a purchase. Across the street is Allison's, which offers a wide selection of photographs and watercolour prints. If it is antique paintings you are seeking, try the House of Falconer, also located on Main Street. As you head east out of town, take the time to appreciate gracious Merrill House bed-and-breakfast, identified by what must be the tallest gables in all of Ontario.

Just east of Picton on Highway 33 is Don Dawson's Willow Studio. This is a pleasant spot to stop and chat about art. Dawson works in a variety of media, from wood to oils, but it's his laboriously produced coloured-pencil drawings that really catch the eye. Whether the subject is a Grecian landscape or racehorses pounding around a curve, this is art worth relishing.

And now on to the last studio of the day. It may seem like a long drive to Black Creek and Denise Belanger-Taylor, but the scenery

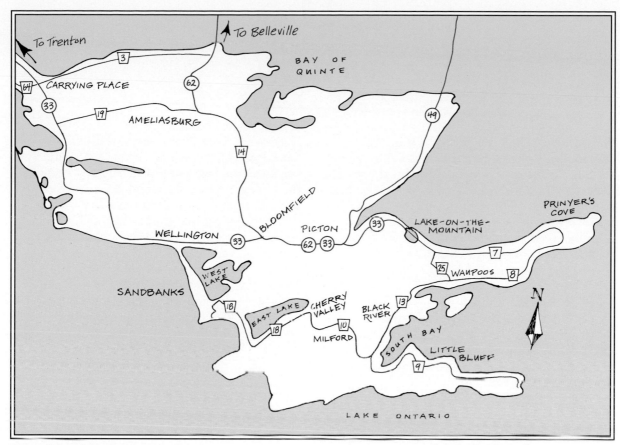

Prince Edward County

is lovely and the studio is well worth the effort. From the Willow Studio, follow Highway 33 (and later, Country Road 7) east; turn south on Road 25 and then west on Country Road 13. Once you enter the village of Black Creek (with its famous cheese factory), turn down Morrison's Point Road. It's a 2-kilometre drive to the studio of glass blower Belanger-Taylor.

It's no wonder that her works have earned the artist an avid international following— they are simply beyond compare. Vases, plant pots, jewellery cases and perfume bottles with the strength of glass and yet of great delicacy are created in a kaleidoscope of colours. Glass plates decorated with landscape designs make an especially effective display when the light coming through the window is of the same sunset tints. A fitting end to a day of great beauty and craftsmanship.

Whether it's the clarity of a well-taken photograph, the rich tones of a century-old landscape painting or the magical way hand-blown glass plays with light, Prince Edward County has more quality art to appreciate— and purchase—than any other spot in Ontario.

> Most galleries open daily during summer; hours vary during winter

11

PICTON
A Joy to Behold

If you have a high regard for a beautiful landscape, Prince Edward County is a joy to behold. The county encompasses a variety of scenery, from farmyard to seascape, all within a compact area. This trip travels the southern half of Prince Edward County (Quinte's Isle) in a clockwise direction. A detailed local road map will be a help, and you may want to refer to the map for trip 10.

Begin on County Road 7 east of Picton, at Lake-on-the-Mountain Provincial Park. Although our smallest provincial park, this spot presents visitors with an intriguing mix of mystery and serenity. Lake-on-the-Mountain rests 62 metres above Lake Ontario, carved out of the limestone bedrock by glacial meltwater. From there is a panoramic view

of the dark waters and tiny green islands of Adolphus Reach, which separates Quinte's Isle from the mainland. Far below your feet the Glenora ferry, slow and silent, moves between mainland Ontario and the island. The view is soothing and not much changed since it captured the imagination of settlers a couple of centuries ago.

Now cross the roadway and climb up the boardwalk to view infamous Lake-on-the-Mountain itself. Exhibits highlight the significance of the lake in natural history and folklore. The still waters were revered by Mohawks. Early settlers, puzzled because the lake had no obvious source and because the lake's level rose and fell in exact concordance with that of Lake Erie, concluded that the

Sandbanks Provincial Park

two bodies were mysteriously connected. Unromantic geologists hypothesize that the lake is fed by local ground water through fissures in its bedrock base.

From the provincial park drive east along County Road 7 to Prinyer's Cove, where the United Empire Loyalists first landed. Today the cove is a snug harbour for sailboats. Backtrack to signposted Bongard Crossroad and head south through orchards fragrantly beautiful during spring blossom. The county's trademark red barns and the lush pastures dotted with contented sheep make this drive a photographer's dream. It's good for cycling, too, with almost no traffic and level roadways in perfect condition.

Turn west onto County Road 8, which you will follow through to Waupoos, where the Rose House Museum details the settlement of this locality, the oldest and most beautiful part of the county. You may choose to eat at the Duke of Marysburgh pub, or buy the makings of a picnic at the general store. Keep driving west along Lake Ontario; the road becomes County Road 13. At South Bay, explore the Mariner's Museum; the landmark 1828 lighthouse was relocated here from False Ducks Island. The waters in the vicinity are known as the graveyard of Lake Ontario and the museum is filled to the gunwales with items such as a pirate's strongbox, Spanish pieces-of-eight and a variety of historic nautical gear.

Continue east along the coastal road to breezy Little Bluff Conservation Area for a sweeping view from high atop limestone cliffs. All that lies below is a narrow cobblestone beach. All that stretches to the horizon is Lake Ontario, either summery blue or wintry grey.

If the museum has you eager to experience more of the mariner's life, drive east on County Road 9. Here the farms are conspicuously less prosperous than those on the rest of the island; it's as if the community has turned its back on the land and stares continually towards the sea. But neglect means that lilac, elderberry and wildflowers have taken over the roadside, to the delight of travellers. The road ends with the scene of drying nets, ice huts, fishing tugs and a weather-beaten lighthouse that makes up the tranquil

Prince Edward Point fishing colony. This is the last such community on Lake Ontario.

Retrace your route to County Road 9 and follow it to Road 10, where a leftward turn will take you to Cherry Valley. Turn west here onto County Road 18; this leads to the special treat of the trip, Sandbanks Provincial Park.

Sandbanks is divided into two sections, East Lake and West Lake. The scenery buff will head for the West Lake area to see the world's largest fresh-water sand-dune system. The magnificent result of 12,000 years of glaciation, water and wind, the dunes are 20-metre mountains of white sand fringed with wild grasses and poplar. A wide-angle view from the peaks takes in both Lake Ontario and quiet West Lake; the only marks on the dunes will be your own footprints. The scene is appealingly wild at dusk, when fox, nighthawks, and frogs add their voices to the wind's song.

Activity abounds in the park's East Lake sector, where the vast beach has space for one and all. The wind and waves are rated top-notch by boardsailors, and there are rentals and instruction. East Lake is the focus of park naturalist programs and you'll find the activities organized for children especially good. Take the opportunity to explore the nature centre, hiking trails and the travelling "dune cart" to find out more about Sandbanks' unusual natives, such as brook lobelia orchids, silver-haired bats and wolf spiders.

Prince Edward County is a beauty spot beyond compare. The only compensation for those leaving the island is that the next daytrip will reveal only more of Prince Edward's diverse charm.

Mariner's Museum
Mid-May to mid-October:
Saturday & Sunday 9:00-5:00
July & August:
Daily 9:00-5:00
Closed Fridays
(613) 476-4695

Sandbanks and Lake-on-the-Mountain
Provincial Parks
(613) 393-3319

BON ECHO PROVINCIAL PARK
Gibraltar of Ontario

The towering granite cliffs that overlook the narrows of a northern lake have provided a moniker for Bon Echo Provincial Park: the Gibraltar of Ontario. The park has such a unique combination of human history and natural majesty that it is, for many, a cherished favourite among our provincial parks. Bon Echo is located at Highway 41 about 30 kilometres north of Kaladar.

Bon Echo's distinctiveness began about a billion years ago, when molten rock from the earth's interior began to cool. Immense forces tilted the rock in a process geologists call "faulting." A fault line runs through Bon Echo; the eastern section rose to form spectacular Mazinaw Rock and the western side sank into very deep Mazinaw Lake.

Bon Echo's famous rock has attracted attention over the span of human history. Red ochre Native Indian pictographs—rock paintings—are located on the rock near water level. There is no theory as to their message or significance, but they continue to draw visitors from far and wide. Much later, Mazinaw became the site of an expensive and exclusive resort hotel. Built in the late nineteenth century, the hotel was bought by Mrs. Flora Denison, and she turned the resort into a shrine to poet Walt Whitman. That accounts for the memorial including lines of poetry cut into the face of Mazinaw Rock. Both pictographs and poetry must be seen by boat. The hotel burned in the 1930s, but the site and some outbuildings remain on the wooded slopes opposite the famous rock.

This 114-metre plunge of striated rock into the lake may be Bon Echo's most famous site, but it is not only geology that makes Bon Echo of interest to students of nature. Because Bon Echo is located where northern (Canadian Shield) habitat and southern, mixed-forest habitat overlap, the park is home to a great diversity of plants and animals. Moose, wolf and spruce are at the southern end of their range, while the turkey vulture,

five-lined skink (Ontario's only indigenous lizard) and oaks are at the northern most edge of their range. All of these species, and many more, can be found in the park.

You'll have to decide how best to appreciate Bon Echo's special beauty, on foot or by canoe or boat, since the park offers excellent facilities for each mode of transport.

Four principal hiking trails range in length from 1 to 17 kilometres; there is also a 2.4-kilometre fitness trail. The Bon Echo Creek Trail follows a small creek, and is an excellent place to introduce children to kingfishers, turtles and frogs. The two intermediate-length trails are called High Pines and Shield. The former is a pleasant walk through forest of hemlock and pine and is highlighted with an overlook of Mazinaw Rock; the latter is a 4.8-kilometre hike through rugged, rocky Canadian Shield country that includes portions of an abandoned colonization road. For the true backwoods hiker, the Abes and Essens Trail (brochure available) is made up of three loops that total 17 kilometres. This is a full-day hike, or you can reserve the walk-in wilderness campsites en route if you want an overnighter. Most trails have interpretive brochures describing points of interest.

For canoeists, there is the Kishkebus Canoe Trail (brochure available). This is a day-long, 21-kilometre paddle beginning at Mazinaw Rock with four portages, including a long carry between Mazinaw and Kishkebus lakes. Sights along the way include Indian pictographs, the Whitman memorial, a maple-yellow birch grove with trees up to one metre in diameter, the carnivorous pitcher plant and osprey. Bon Echo has many fine, quiet lakes for paddling; motorboats are prohibited on all but Mazinaw and Joeperry lakes. The Mississippi Canoe route is for the serious paddler: it takes about one week to travel, following a river and lake. Canoes and other equipment may be rented or

Bon Echo Rock, Bon Echo Provincial Park.

purchased at outfitters located just south of the park gates.

A third option is the Mugwump ferry, which runs daily during the summer to carry visitors to the base of Mazinaw Rock. A trail, including stairs, allows access to the top and a spectacular view. A second ferry tour (90 minutes) covers Upper and Lower Mazinaw lakes.

Even without a boat you can come face-to-face with the cliffs by walking along the shoreline near the marina. A narrow channel of about 10 metres separates you from the sheer cliff-face. The rock is streaked with grey, red and green, cedars cling to crevices, and turkey vultures soar overhead. The bench here is a great spot to sit and admire the rock and watch the many boaters navigate through the passage.

You do not need to be an energetic hiker or canoeist to enjoy Bon Echo. The campground has two very good beaches. There is a nature interpretation program that includes walks and amphitheatre plays; displays on the natural and human history of the region are located in a cottage that dates to the Denison resort. Fishing for pickerel, pike, perch and lake trout is a popular pastime here.

There is enough natural diversity and spectacular scenery at Bon Echo to last a lifetime of daytrips, as any park enthusiast will tell you. Add your name to the list of historical characters who have come to admire the Gibraltar of Ontario.

Bon Echo Provincial Park
(613) 336-2228

Smart's Marina
(canoe rentals)
(613) 336-2222

KALADAR
The Artland of Ontario

Make no mistake about it: the region around Kaladar, where Highways 7 and 41 intersect, is a hot-bed of galleries and studios, all featuring exceptional works. Why here, well off the beaten track? Perhaps the diverse landscape, a mix of bucolic farmland and rugged forest, is the source of inspiration. Whatever the reason, those looking for a special piece to start, or expand a collection will want to take this daytrip. (Don't forget to pack your road map.)

Scout out this area by beginning at tiny Arden, tucked away in cottage country near Big Clear Lake. Drive south from Highway 7 about 2.5 kilometres along County Road 15. Arden Batik is located in the centre of town and welcomes visitors. Though traditionally known as a waxing and dyeing technique used to create brilliantly coloured clothing, Sarah Hale uses batik to capture the beauty of the Canadian Shield. Hale's work comes in the form of inexpensive cards or large wall hangings. It's also nice to meet the artist behind the work as you browse.

Drive west along Highway 7 to Highway 41 and turn north. The next village is Northbrook, where you'll find Treadles Tea Room, Sandy Beach Antiques, and Strokes craft shop— housed together as Creative Impressions. Treadles serves light meals in a renovated church; Sandy Beach sells antiques, and has an intriguing collection of piano rolls, menus, maps, postcards and music; Strokes provides abundant supplies and instruction in tole and other decorator arts. From Northbrook return to Highway 7 and head west.

Studio 737 (on Highway 7 about 20 kilometres west of Highway 41) has earned a reputation as the largest private collection of fine art in Canada. Schedule plenty of time to peruse the hundreds of oils, watercolours, pen-and-ink sketches, pastels, and sculpture in wood, stone and clay. All works are originals by over 60 prominent, or soon-to-be prominent, artists. One room is devoted to

Canadian "Old Masters" such as Masson. Throughout the 10 rooms at Studio 737 the subject matter is distinctly Canadian, from rocky countryside to city back-alleys to portraits of east-coast fishermen. Arja Palonen, artist-in-residence, is often in the studio at work and her husband, Joe Kurek, is an expert at framing, which makes this a good spot to seek advice on art collection, framing and art supplies.

Drive east on Highway 7 to where it intersects with Highway 41. (You may wish to stop en route at the studio of Paul Thrane, whose work may be seen at Studio 737.) Turn south on 41, and then east on County Road 4, towards Tamworth. This tranquil village with a delightful "downtown" park is home to the studio of A. J. (Bert) Vermeulen. His watercolours and oils cover a wide range of subjects, from reflective lakes to townscapes, and he has abstract paintings as well. Across the street, the Five Corners Craft Centre is a good place to catch an overview of local works, including painting, carving, pottery and ceramics, weaving and quilting. There's an especially good selection of hand-knit sweaters. Right next door is the Devon Tea Room. A relaxed and homey atmosphere pervades, and the choices on the menu range from lasagna to soup and sandwiches.

Return to Highway 41 and drive just north to County Road 13. Head west through Marlbank. On the west end of town, follow signs to Philoxia, one of Eastern Ontario's most unusual sites. What is Philoxia? Well, it's a community whose philosophy and lifestyle integrates ideas from a mix of ancient cultures. The public is invited to enjoy the restaurant, craft shop and small zoo. (Modest admission charged.)

Begin with the zoo, a refuge for animals that cannot be housed in regular zoos. There are wolves, lions, tigers, rhea (affectionately named Null, Void and Ditto for their apparent lack of intelligence), rabbits and a

Creative Impressions, Northbrook.

variety of deer and llamas. The large and lazy bear gives toothless greetings to whoever wishes a warm and wet lick. Best of all are the monkeys, in several species, sizes and colours. Hand-feeding the monkeys, a popcorn morsel or peanut at a time, will surely make the day of any child. It provides a special close-up look, and feel, of tiny monkey hands and faces.

Philoxia runs a restaurant (weekends only) that serves macrobiotic and vegan-vegetarian meals. The varied menu includes three-grain burgers, fettucini and a variety of fish dishes. The emphasis is on interpretations of Middle Eastern and Slavic foods. On Saturday evenings there are banquets, complete with gypsy music. Visitors with an interest in shiatsu or reiki massage, macro-cooking or a spiritual retreat can book for an extended

stay, which includes swimming, skiing and other sports facilities.

The craft shop sells marvellous rocking horses and other wooden toys, homemade beeswax candles and recordings of Philoxia's own musicians.

If you love art but are shy of the big-city art world, then come to the countryside surrounding Kaladar for a real treat: the chance to shop for top-notch works at reasonable prices, in quiet surroundings.

Philoxia
Restaurant open for lunch
weekends mid-June to September
Saturday buffet 6:00
Zoo open daily year-round
(613) 478-6070

14

EGANVILLE
Children's Corner

Renfrew County is a great region for daytripping families because children can enjoy a variety of experiences without having to drive long distances. Far from the crowds and high prices of the big city and located in a vast landscape of forest and water, Renfrew provides visitors a day of caves, waterslides and family entertainment.

From Ottawa, drive north on Highway 17. A few kilometres north of Renfrew, watch for signs indicating the eastward turn to Storyland Road; it's another 4 kilometres from Highway 17 to the park. Storyland is a great place for young children. They can wander along wooded paths to encounter 200 storybook characters in about 25 scenes; some of the characters are animated and at the press of a button, will spin a story, wave, wink, or sing a song.

Professional puppeteers present shows several times daily, and there are often special events, for example, Canada's birthday party. Activities include mini-golf, roller racers (also known as flying turtles, an exercise apparatus popular with kids but perhaps a novelty to parents), paddleboats and traditional playground equipment. The sweeping view of the Ottawa River and the green mountains of Quebec is worth the low price of admission (about the same as taking the family to the cinema), and includes all activities. Families may bring a picnic or fill up at the snack bar or restaurant.

A couple of hours at Storyland will leave the little ones content to sit in the car as you head for the Bonnechere Caves, situated between Douglas and Eganville. (Return to Highway 17, drive south to Renfrew and

Bonnechere Caves, between Douglas and Eganville.

take Highway 60 northwest to Douglas. At the Bank of Montreal follow the sign that indicates a left turn; the caves are about 4 kilometres from town.)

The story of the Bonnechere Caves takes us back millions of years to the origins of our land, when a warm inland sea covered what is now the Ottawa Valley. Deposits of limestone were formed from the skeletons of countless sea creatures, and this limestone was slowly dissolved by rain and glacial water to form underground caverns or surface depressions. When this erosion occurs along fault-lines in the rock, narrow, winding underground corridors are created, decorated with weirdly-shaped stalactites and stalagmites, and streaked with iron (red), magnesium (blue) or calcium (white).

Take the guided tour, a wonderful subterranean adventure. You'll be grateful that the caverns have been left au naturel and not altered to produce gimmicky effects as seen in many other locations. The passageway twists along an old watercourse, and the corridor walls are sculpted and fluted by the force of water. At some points the track is so narrow that shoulders (or heads!) are scraped on the dripping rock face. Sometimes the pathway opens into large "parlours," formed by spinning whirlpool waters, where guides stop to discuss geology—you'll learn how to judge water velocity and depth, and how to tell the age of a stalactite.

Most fascinating of all are the extraordinary adventures of spelunker Tom Woodward, who explored the caves in the 1950s, and installed pumps to lower water-levels. Visitors take away a vivid impression of the danger and difficulties facing Woodward, as he encountered raging torrents, bats, and of course, complete darkness. Visitors get a taste of that blackness when the guide turns off the lights—but don't worry, in a few moments the group leaves the underground world and returns to the starting point by way of a steep, ferny glen.

The Bonnechere River valley is good fossil-hunting ground, and visitors are encouraged to try their luck. Children love searching around for a brachiopod, trilobite or piece of ancient coral. Adults simply enjoy the view of the tumbling river, named at this point

Fourth Chute, since this is the fourth set of waterfalls and rapids upstream from the Ottawa River.

Head into Eganville, where there are several eateries to choose from. The Granary Restaurant serves authentic Austrian cuisine such as schnitzel and rouladen, as well as burgers and sandwiches. Verch's Bakery and the Peaches and Cream Dairy Bar can outfit a family with take-away goodies to be enjoyed at Centennial Park, perched high above the river (access by a long bridge near the tourist information centre).

The last stop of the day is Logosland, located on Highway 17 just southeast of Cobden. While Storyland is best suited to younger children, Logosland will appeal to the active older kids. Waterslides (in two sizes, giant and kiddie), walking and biking trails, adventure playgrounds, paddleboats, mini-golf and horseback riding are guaranteed to exercise any child. There is a cafeteria and gift shop in the building modelled after Noah's Ark.

Whether travelling with a van full of children, or only with those who are young at heart, visitors to Renfrew County agree that this is Ontario's "children's corner."

Storyland
Mid-May to mid-June:
Daily 10:00-5:00
(weekdays limited facilities)
Mid-June to September:
Daily 9:30-6:00
September to mid-October:
Sunday 10:00-5:00
(613) 432-5275

Bonnechere Caves
Mid-May to July:
Daily 10:00-4:00
July & August:
Daily 9:00-5:00
Mid-September to mid-October:
Saturday & Sunday 10:00-4:00
(613) 628-2002

Logosland (waterpark)
Mid-June to September:
Daily 10:00-7:00
(613) 646-2313

15

PEMBROKE
In Champlain's Footsteps

The mighty Ottawa River pervades life along its banks. Throughout the area around Pembroke the river's eminence is celebrated through art, museums and tourist attractions. Join in the tribute by travelling to Pembroke for a day down by the riverside.

The most famous Ottawa River traveller was Champlain himself who, in 1613, was the first European to explore the site that is now Pembroke. His reputation lives on at the Champlain Trail Museum. Located at the south end of town on Pembroke Street (the main street), the museum comprises several buildings, including a log pioneer homestead, fire station and one-room schoolhouse. The main exhibit hall has a wide range of artifacts, maps and text describing local fossil finds, Indian life, fur trading and the voyageurs. The glory days of Ottawa Valley logging are covered in the greatest detail, with exhibits on logging tools and methods, life in the lumber camps, the treacherous river rapids, and the types and grades of valley timber.

Head downtown for an appealing eyeful of riverside life, proudly displayed in huge and expertly painted murals on over a dozen downtown buildings. Each mural is painted in a different style, and they make for a fascinating downtown stroll; an explanatory brochure is available from town hall and downtown merchants. Here are a few of the scenes from Pembroke's history you can find in the murals: there's Champlain himself (the mural is designed as four paintings on a Victorian wall), the logging industry (a lovely sepia tone, pictured as a page from an artist's sketchbook), pointer boats on the river, the riverside icehouse, Pembroke streetlights (this was the first town in Canada with commercial electric streetlights), rafting then and now (logging rafts and modern whitewater rafts), and local Hockey Hall of Famers.

Another mural portrays Pembroke as Canada's Capistrano. Each year in early August, tens of thousands of swallows gather along the river near Pembroke before beginning their southward migration. Birdwatchers (also in great numbers and from far and wide) are drawn to this natural attraction. The exact site of the swallow party changes from year to year (although it is often across the bay from the marina), so consult town hall for the current best sighting spot.

After stopping to appreciate the indescribably blue river from the vantage point of the town marina (foot of Albert Street), travel south out of town along Highway 148. Follow signs to cross over the bridge to Quebec. The view from the bridge is the reason for this short detour—it allows you a 180-degree sweep of river. Return to the Ontario side and drive south along County Road 21; keep as close to the river as possible, turning along County Roads 12 and 43. (A road map would be a good idea!)

The landscape is one of typical Ottawa Valley family farms, hay-scented fields, log barns, and the river plays a game of hide-and-seek with the traveller. Sleepy little villages dominated by churches with tall, silver steeples mark the crossroads, and you'll come across the occasional fishing resort. Eventually, you will see signs for the whitewater rafting companies that maintain facilities on the river just east of Beachburg and Forester's Falls.

Follow the signs to end up at Wilderness Tours headquarters. The restaurant here is called Rafters, and it is the best bet for a meal today. Not only is the food ample (manicotti, falafel and roast beef, for example) and reasonably priced, but this is one exciting place to soak up a riverside atmosphere. Dripping wet after a trip, rafters sit side-by-side with kayakers and canoeists, discussing rapids with ominous names such as Butcherknife, Black Chute, and Hell's Half Mile. (Check out the back of the menu for the chilling details.) It feels like a beach club, with a constant flow of fit and bronzed young

Detail of Champlain mural, Pembroke.

people heading out for volleyball, mountain biking, horseback riding or bungee-jumping (before lunch, one presumes). The centre of the restaurant is the bar, where overhead video screens play a continuous show of foaming white-water rafting, power boating and kayaking. For the timid, this may be as close to the action as you want to get.

There's a different, and equally appealing, atmosphere at the Owl Rafting headquarters. The clientele includes lots of young people, but also many families, since Owl will take kids as young as eight years of age on the Ottawa. Budget-priced day-care is provided for those too young to raft. As at Wilderness Tours, rafting packages at Owl can be for a full day with meals, or for weekend adventures, and can include a variety of on-shore recreation activities.

After having gained some respect for the Ottawa, whether through the eyes of hardy voyageurs or modern daredevils, it's time to head downstream and home. The route along County Roads 3 and 4 includes some wonderful views of the river and forested hills. Enjoy.

Champlain Trail Museum
Early April to mid-May
and mid-September to December:
Monday-Friday 10:00-5:00
Mid-May to September:
Monday-Saturday 10:00-5:00
Sunday 1:30-5:00
Closed Tuesdays year-round
(613) 735-0517

Wilderness Tours
(613) 646-2291

Owl Rafting
(613) 646-2263

NAPANEE
Down by the Old Mill Stream

A history of Ontario's early European inhabitants must focus on the rivers, that acted as transportation and settlement corridors and provided energy for countless mills. Many rivers have had their early history obliterated by urban development; fortunately, for the daytripper, the valley of the Napanee River retains much of its historic charm.

A Napanee River excursion properly begins at the county seat, Napanee. Right in the centre of town is one of Ontario's oldest town halls (1856). The building and surroundings were designed to resemble an American-style hall and town commons. From town hall, walk or drive two blocks north to Thomas Street and turn east. Continue along Thomas to the two massive and rugged limestone buildings: the Lennox and Addington County Court (with a dome and pillars) and the County Jail. The jail is now a museum and archives, and few local history museums are so neatly and professionally arranged. Maps, dioramas, and domestic, farm and industrial artifacts present county history from Woodland Indians through to modern times; much of the focus is on the local settlement and history of the United Empire Loyalists.

One such Loyalist was Scot Allan Macpherson, who was justice of the peace and owned mills, a distillery and general store. His 1826 home on First Street (go east on Thomas two blocks from the museum) is an exemplary white frame Georgian building with picket-fence charm. The period gardens overlook a particularly pretty stretch of the Napanee River. Personable, costumed Macpherson House guides provide tours covering the fully furnished morning room, parlour, office, kitchen, bedrooms and ballroom. Macpherson House hosts special events and activities, including cream teas each Thursday afternoon during the summer.

Now it's time to head up that old mill stream. From Macpherson House, head north along Camden Road (County Road 1). The next Napanee mill town encountered is Newburgh. With its steep hills and shaded streets of stone homes and stores, this is a perfect picture of quiet, small-town Ontario. In days past, Newburgh was a busy village boasting dozens of mills and factories and the Newburgh Academy, a teachers' college, which still stands at the west end of the village. Much of the town was destroyed by fires in 1887, 1902 and 1908, and it never regained its former bustle. Take a riverside walk in Newburgh Conservation Area near the bridge.

Continue along Road 1 towards Camden East. Its nineteenth-century mills may have vanished, but Camden East is experiencing a revival, thanks to the presence of Harrowsmith and Equinox magazines and Camden House Books. These publishing enterprises have brought some employment and a lot of travellers to the village. A visit to the Camden House bookshop is a good pilgrimage for those interested in stunning books on country life, gardening, self-sufficiency and nature.

Camden East's Riverside Drive, just downhill from the bookshop, is a pleasant detour. The road follows the river's shallow, brown water as it skips over limestone shelves. If it's time for a meal, try the Oats 'n Honey bed-and-breakfast just south of town, which serves delicious vegetarian meals. For a good taste of life in the slow lane, enjoy an ample serving of fresh strawberry shortcake on the deck overlooking the river.

Journey upstream to pretty Yarker. Yarker is home to the Waterfall Tea Room and the Wonderful Store. A small selection of vegetarian meals is served in a room with a view of the river and mill ruins; the noise of the falls fills the room. The store offers antiques, paintings and a good selection of used books. Along the street at the top of the hill is Old Church Cottage Antiques. It is worth a visit to marvel at the restored church and its pointy Gothic windows.

Waterfall Tea Room, Yarker.

Retrace your route along County Road 1 and at County Road 6, head south. (This path takes us out of the Napanee Valley, but it is for good reason, as you shall see.) At County Road 20, turn east and follow signs to Wilton. Stop at the Wilton Cheese factory for a tasty souvenir of cheddar or cream cheese. Wilton Pottery is popular for its high-quality functional and decorative porcelain and stoneware. Return to County Road 6 and follow it south to Odessa.

You are now in the watershed of Millhaven Creek at Odessa, which began life, as all the towns visited today, as a mill town. From the main street of town, turn down Bridge Street to the mill. Odessa is very fortunate to have a fully operational water-powered mill that uses original machinery to produce "Better Baskets by Babcock."

The mill was constructed in 1850 as a grist mill. In 1908 the Babcock family turned it into a basket mill, using its patented Babcock basket design. Highly informative and detailed tours are given of the mill and the basket-

making process. Beautiful maple baskets, from picnic size to laundry hamper size, are available. Purchase a basket to hold your souvenirs of the day and to serve as a reminder of mill life in the nineteenth century.

Lennox and Addington County Museum and Archives
Monday-Friday 10:00-4:30
(613) 354-3027

Allan Macpherson House
March-December:
Monday-Friday 12:00-4:30
July & August:
Wednesday-Sunday 9:30-4:30
(613) 354-5982

Babcock Mill
Late June to September:
Thursday-Monday 10:00-4:00
(613) 306-7060 summer
(613) 389-8314 winter

BARRYVALE
A Kick and Push into Summer

Lanark County contains two exceptional destinations sure to gladden the heart of any nature-lover: the K & P Trail and the Purdon Conservation Area. Both sites usher in the balmy days of late spring and early summer with a profusion of blooms and a symphony of bird song. Watch the weather and prepare for a bright, outdoorsy day in Lanark.

The trip starts in the cottage-country town of Calabogie (pack a good road map). You will want to reach town via Highway 508, which meanders along the Madawaska River, at this point flowing wide and peaceful. Travel south from Calabogie on Highway 511 and follow signs to Barryvale, located 5 kilometres off 511. Those expecting a humble backwoods hamlet will be surprised to encounter a

modern golf resort complete with condos. The road ends at the shore of Calabogie Lake and the beginning of the K & P Trail.

The 40-kilometre gravel trail runs along an abandoned railway right-of-way from which it takes its name, the Kingston and Pembroke Railway (affectionately called the Kick and Push Line). Trains ran from the late 1800s to the 1950s, carrying timber south to Kingston and settlers north to the hinterland. Much to its credit, the Mississippi Valley Conservation Authority maintains the trail for the enjoyment of hikers, bikers, snowmobilers and skiers. The trail is manageable by car, although a four-wheel-drive vehicle would be an advantage because portions of the trail are sometimes water-logged. Travel by mountain

Near Calabogie.

bike or foot allows the fullest appreciation of this unique trail.

Some will want to travel the entire line from Barryvale south to Snow Road Station. Many will want to see just the most scenic stretch, which is the northern half. There are fire pits, privies, shelters and parking lots along the trail. (Excellent maps are available from the conservation authority.) The scenery is the typical, but exhilarating, stuff Northern Ontario is made of: wetlands with beaver lodges, kingfishers and lily pads; mixed forest of birch, poplar and white pine; rock cuts through granite sparkling white, black and pink. Bridges traverse small creeks and afford good chances for a photograph. You slow your stride, the better to enjoy the sweet air and revitalizing serenity.

If you are trekking only the northern portion of the trail, return to Barryvale. There are two restaurants, the Highlands and Barryvale Lodge. Barryvale has the best view of Calabogie Lake and a more diverse menu. Closer to Calabogie, the Calabogie Resort and Conference Centre serves a Sunday brunch. Those travelling the complete trail will end up in Snow Road Station on Highway 509. Stop along the way to appreciate the small railroad village of Lavant Station. (There is a small store en route at Flower Station.) If you are coming from Barryvale, travel back to Highway 511 and turn south. Turn west at Country Road 8 (towards Watsons Corners). Follow signs north to Purdon Conservation Area. If travelling from Snow Road Station, use a good road map to navigate the back roads to Purdon.

Purdon Conservation Area is unusual in that it contains several different types of wetland: marsh, swamp, and fen. It is the fen that is of the greatest interest, famous as having the largest colony of showy lady's-slipper orchids in Canada. About 16,000 delicate white and rosy-pink orchids go into glorious bloom in late June or early July. The peak bloom time is usually around Father's Day in June, but weather conditions affect flowering, so consult with the conservation authority near the time of your trip.

There is one trail with two access points, one that includes a lookout over Purdon Lake, and another that is designed to be wheelchair accessible. Use either one to see the spectacular show of flowers, down at the bottom of steep wooded slopes. Self-guiding interpretive brochures are often available from the rack near the parking lot but to ensure you have one, contact the conservation authority.

The fen is carefully managed to create the best possible conditions for the flowers. That means controlling water levels, thinning tree cover, transplanting orchids to the best locations and protecting the plants from pickers. This effort was pioneered by original owner Joe Purdon, who began work on the colony in the 1930s; some of the plants you are enjoying today are almost 60 years old.

It is difficult to miss out on a fine display of spring flowers at Purdon, since it is also home to leafy white bog orchid, marsh blue violet, the carnivorous pitcher plant, blue flag iris, and many ferns and grasses. Those who appreciate animals will be on the lookout for beaver (their dam provides for natural water-level regulation), heron, ducks and many kinds of woodland birds.

There's nothing like a nature ramble to revive senses dulled by weeks of life indoors. And there is no better way to appreciate spring blossoming into summer than by visiting the K & P Trail and Purdon Conservation Area.

Mississippi Valley Conservation Authority
(613) 259-2421

19

RENFREW
The Towns That Lumber Built

Big timber country: tales of log booms and mill wheels, lumberjacks and timber barons permeate the culture of Ontario. Visit Renfrew and Arnprior, where the lumber drive and vast fortunes made from trees are still within living memory, and where dark green forests and historic lumber towns live in scenic harmony.

Drive west from Ottawa along Highway 17, and exit at Highway 60 to arrive in Renfrew. Follow the main street of town, Raglan Street (it changes to Stewart Street), to Arthur Avenue and the McDougall Mill Museum. This three-storey grey-stone building is located above the chasm of the Bonnechere River, where the water churns and spills its way over boulders. (Picnickers will find the tables at the museum an ideal site.)

The museum is devoted to early commerce and domestic life in "the Valley." Home life is represented by a fine collection of clothing, from wedding gowns to hockey uniforms; pictures, spinning wheels, dolls and quilts round out the exhibit. Another floor is devoted to farm implements, sleighs and, of course, early logging and woodworking tools such as saws, carts and stump removers.

Now return along Raglan Street to downtown Renfrew. On the way, take a short detour along Munroe to Lorne Street to find the Centreside Dairy. This is the home of Tracey's Old Fashioned Recipe Ice Cream, favoured by connoisseurs throughout the valley. You won't be disappointed by the taste of raspberry chocolate macaroon, Heath Bar crunch or any of the other 65 flavours.

And then it's back to the main street. Many of the stores and theatres along Raglan were built by families made rich by lumber, and the small-town charm has been altered little during the past century. The fascinating and tangled history of local lumber millionaires, or barons, is unravelled at the Old Town Hall Tea Room, built in 1893. Tea (what else for the former temperance hall?), scones, sandwiches and Sunday brunch are served, and newspaper articles displayed on the walls will fill you in on local legends.

The lumber boom years of the late 1800s spawned several heroes; familiar names include O'Brien, Barnet and Carswell. So much money was to be made from the surrounding forest that the local hockey team, which competed for the 1910 Stanley Cup, was named the "Millionaires." Four houses built by O'Brien sit on "Millionaire's Corner," now the intersection of Quarry and Barr. (From Raglan, take Renfrew Street to Quarry.) Number 277 Barr was a wedding gift from O'Brien to his daughter. Number 154 Quarry, constructed with curved walls, was intended for O'Brien himself, but the house was sold when his wife refused to leave the original family home at 247 Barnet. Bid adieu to Renfrew and head for another town made rich during the heyday of lumber—Arnprior. Lumber baron Daniel McLachlin constructed a mill here in the mid-1800s, as did the four Gillies brothers.

The Arnprior and District Museum, which sits on the main intersection of town, is a red sandstone building with a brightly coloured roof that is so flamboyant, it's a traffic-stopper. The museum records Arnprior's history from its days as a feudal fiefdom under Laird McNab to modern times. Along with items from stores and homes, the exhibit includes an excellent collection of photographs, maps and memoirs from early logging camps.

Arnprior celebrates the 1860 trip of King Edward VII to visit Daniel McLachlin, and the "treasure vault" room contains many personal items of the monarch, including the famous tiepin lost, and found, in Arnprior. The top floor of the museum, the tower room, provides a view over town and the confluence of the Ottawa and Madawaska rivers.

and th...
downfa...
Templ...
used by...
congreg...
schoolh...
served...
mid-18(...
implem...
carpenti...

Conside...
spacious...
shores ...
any sea:...
head ba...
Stirling...
built thi...
as the v...
House c...
restaurar...
region—...
homema...
(for exar...
and Stilt...
risotto o...
pastries ...
plum tar...
zucotta ...

And nov...
from Wh...
entrance...
and very...
The fall...
In a regic...
colour, th...

Tiny Bur...
tourists g...
that you...
The gift ...
exception...
the shopk...
itself prett...

First off, ...
everything...
home crai...
tole suppli...
dried flow...

McDougall Mill Museum, Renfrew.

It was at the mouth of the Madawaska River that McLachlin built a large sawmill. That waterfront is now Robert Simpson Park, a pleasant place to survey the wide Ottawa River. Although the busy traffic of steamboats and log booms no longer make the river the main street of town, the river's calm surface is occasionally creased by a pleasure craft from the municipal marina. Just beside the park and hidden from view by trees is the original mansion built by Daniel McLachlin; it is now a religious institution.

There is one more stop in the vicinity relating to the glory years of Ottawa Valley lumber. Drive out of Arnprior northwest along River Road (ask for directions at the museum). A few kilometres out of town is the Gillies Brothers and Company Mill, still in operation and identified by the historic plaque at the front entrance, as well as by the gargantuan piles of sawdust and logs. Take the time to appreciate the fine view of the river. It is very wide at this point and intensely blue; gulls swoop overhead and fishermen sit near logs cast up perhaps a century ago.

Whoever said that Canadian history was boring needs to visit the Ottawa Valley towns of Renfrew and Arnprior for a lesson in pioneer life, lumber millionaires—and even some of the best ice cream in the province.

McDougall Mill Museum
June-September:
Daily 9:30-4:30
(613) 432-2129

Arnprior and District Museum
Mid-June to mid-September:
Tuesday-Friday 12:00-5:00
Saturday & Sunday 1:00-4:00
(613) 623-4902

KINGSTON
Cast Off for Kingston

Ahoy, matey! If you hanker for a taste of the big water and crave a sailor's life, then set a course for Kingston. Bounded on three sides by water, the city gained early prominence as a navy shipyard and commercial port. Today, Kingston is a Mecca for fresh-water sailors from around the world. Join them for an enjoyable day on the waterfront.

For an intriguing historical perspective, head for the Marine Museum of the Great Lakes at 55 Ontario Street, on the lakeshore just west of downtown (refer to the map for trip 22). The museum comprises four buildings, part of a shipyard begun in 1790. The dry dock is Ontario's oldest, opened in 1890 by Sir John A. Macdonald. Top-notch displays make the history of navigation on the Great Lakes come alive. The lobby has models and diagrams of freighters, naval vessels and recreational ships from across the centuries, with information on size, weight, engines and speed. There are also displays on the Great Lakes themselves, full of lively details. Did you know that the lakes hold one-fifth of the world's fresh water, enough water to give every person in North America nine baths a day for the rest of their lives?

Changing exhibits highlight special aspects of life on the Great Lakes, for example, shipwrecks (including the tragedy of the *Edmund Fitzgerald*), the era of steam, the Canadian Navy during WWII, and life aboard a Great Lakes freighter. The shipbuilding gallery has very informative documentation and artifacts detailing each stage in the construction process, and the engine room houses the huge engine used to empty the dry dock of water.

The Marine Museum will have you ready to embark on a shipboard adventure. Just exit the front door of the museum and walk up the gangway of the 1959 *Alexander Henry*, a 3,000-ton Coast Guard icebreaker. What a treat it is to scramble all over the ship, exploring the galley, engine room and bridge. A self-guiding brochure will have you using nautical terms with ease (such as forecastle, bulwark, steering flat and promenade deck). It must have been sheer genius that led the museum to run the *Alexander Henry* as a bed-and-breakfast, where guests receive inexpensive lodging in a prime Kingston location. Don't expect delicate decor and room service, but the rooms are shipshape and Bristol fashion (read spare and Spartan but very clean), just as a sailor would expect. The continental breakfast is eaten at a table edged with a rim so that dishes won't fall off in heavy seas.

Just down the street from the museum is the Kingston Pumphouse Steam Museum, in a building originally constructed to supply the city with drinking water. The pumphouse is a museum filled with steam engines, the largest collection of engines run entirely on steam in the world.

From the museum, drive west along Ontario and King streets to Portsmouth Olympic Harbour. The village of Portsmouth is ancient by Ontario standards, and some of the houses have been converted to bed-and-breakfasts, capitalizing on the nautical theme. The Olympic harbour was constructed to host the sailing events of the 1976 Olympics. The facilities are excellent and the challenging winds off Lake Ontario make Kingston the best fresh-water sailing centre in the world. This is the place to charter a yacht—or buy one—and the piers provide a relaxing stroll. The Harbour Restaurant serves burgers and sandwiches or entrees such as crab Tahitian and chicken Kiev.

Backtrack to downtown Kingston. The wharf behind the Holiday Inn is the point of departure for Thousand Islands and Kingston harbour cruises. The harbour cruise on the Island Belle is recommended for today. It leaves twice daily during the summer (phone for exact times and reservations).

The narrated cruises are approximately 90 minutes in length and travel past the mouth of the Cataraqui River and along the length

Main

Alexander Henry Bed and Breakfast, Marine Museum of the Great Lakes.

of Kingston's shoreline to Lake Ontario Park. This a terrific way to see Kingston's lovely sites from a completely different perspective: Fort Henry, the Royal Military College, the city's four defensive Martello towers, City Hall, Confederation Basin, Kingston Penitentiary and Lake Ontario Park. The beaches at the park are a favourite spot for wind-surfing, and no doubt some speed-demon will scoot past during your tour. The cruise is also a good way to pick up some interesting stories from Kingston's past. For example, Canada's first hockey game was played on the ice near Confederation Basin, between RMC and Queen's University.

It may be time for a meal when you return to the wharf. Why not enjoy a waterside view? Drive north on Rideau Street to Cataraqui Street and turn right. At Number 2 is the River Mill Restaurant. An elegant restaurant occupies part of a stone cotton mill constructed in 1880. Menu highlights include swordfish and rack of lamb, followed by homemade ice cream topped with sabayon. The River Mill

is one of the city's more popular spots, so reservations are recommended.

Life on the waterfront, Kingston style, looks very appealing. The next time you need a refreshing day, cast off for Kingston.

Marine Museum of the Great Lakes
April-November:
Daily 10:00-5:00
November-April:
Daily 10:00-4:00
Ship open mid-May to mid-October only
(613) 542-2261

Pumphouse Steam Museum
Mid-May to September:
Daily 10:00-5:00
(613) 546-4696

Island Belle Harbour Cruises
(613) 549-5544

22

KINGSTON
Step in Time

Kingstonians make a lot of claims for their city: the best collection of limestone buildings west of Montreal; the grandest city hall in Ontario; the best-educated and best-fed citizenry of any small city. Good thing they can back up these claims, much to the delight of visitors from near and far.

No doubt about it, Kingston's charm is owed in large measure to its carefully preserved historic district, and the focal point of that district is City Hall, which regally surveys the harbour between Brock and Clarence streets. The architecture is classical in all its symmetrical perfection, with a columned portico, decorated parapets and round dome with four clock faces. There are tours of the equally handsome interior during summer months.

Be sure to visit the tourist information office, located in a refurbished train station in the lively park opposite City Hall. There are downtown walking-tour brochures and information on conducted bike tours (a terrific idea, since local drivers are unexpectedly considerate of cyclists). A tour train provides an hour-long narrated jaunt about the city, starting from the tourist office. Alternatively, take the following exploration.

Immediately behind City Hall is Market Square, bounded by Clarence, King and Brock streets, where a farmers' market began in 1803. The site stills hums with activity each Tuesday, Thursday and Saturday; modern-day vendors have added crafts, jewellery and a profusion of fresh flowers to traditional farm products. There is an antique market on Sundays.

Take a look at the streetscape surrounding the square. Very few cities can boast such uninterrupted lines of nineteenth-century commercial buildings (most were originally hotels). Try the Kingston Brew Pub at 34 Clarence. Calling itself Ontario's first authentic brew pub, this establishment also produces its own wines. In-house standards are real lager and dragon's-breath ale (no

additives); there are also non-alcoholic specialties. The modestly priced menu features substantial sandwiches (bread baked on the premises), fish, steak and chops.

Continue a Kingston tour by walking east along King Street, which has several interesting clothing stores. Kingston's best-loved restaurant, Chez Piggy, is found down an alley running north from King between Brock and Princess. The restaurant itself is a livery stable constructed in 1810. While the butternut-and-pine interior is warmly inviting, don't miss a chance to enjoy the outdoor patio, snuggled in a courtyard surrounded by rough-hewn limestone buildings. You are in the very heart of nineteenth-century Kingston. "Piggy's" clientele is justifiably loyal, since they appreciate a well-prepared meal, from hearty pâtés to luscious desserts, and service that is attentive without being intrusive.

Walk to Brock Street and turn north. On this delightfully narrow street it is easy to imagine away 150 years. While many Brock Street boutiques are interesting, three deserve special attention. Cooke's Old World Shop (59-61) is a veritable cornucopia of internationalgourmet foods. Operating since 1865, Cooke's has made a reputation with fabulous coffees and cheddar cheese. Next door is the Kingston Gallery of Clocks, with dozens of distinctive tickers from imposing grandfather clocks to dainty mantel-top models. The Doll Attic (60) has a complete line of dolls and accessories, including Anne of Green Gables and Madame Alexander dolls and exquisitely furnished doll houses.

Walk north one block on Brock to Wellington and travel west along Wellington and south on Johnson to meet a venerable citizen of Kingston society, St. George's Cathedral. If you have a sense of déjà vu, it may be because one of St. George's domes is modelled after that of St. Paul's Cathedral in London. Originally constructed in 1825, St. George's has seen several major remodellings, but is still a beloved landmark. St. George's choir has a wide international reputation. The

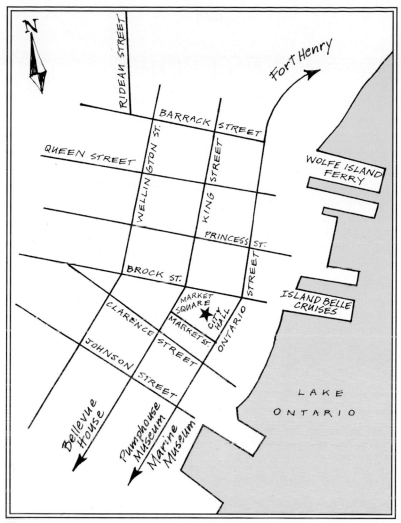

Kingston

colours of the Royal Military College cadets and other military banners adorn the interior.

Opposite St. George's on Johnson Street is Gildersleeve House, home to a shipping magnate of the same name. The home was built in the same year as the cathedral, and is a good example of the residences preferred by Kingston's well-to-do: a plain and symmetrical limestone facade with three windows in the upper storey and a door and two windows on street level. The prosperity of the Gildersleeve family is evidenced by details such as side lights and fanlights in the doorway, arched windows in the gable ends and a cast-iron fence.

Return to your car and drive west along King Street. Turn right at Centre Street to find Bellevue House, the 1848 home of Sir John A. Macdonald. This is a first-rate museum,

with an excellent film on Kingston's history and the development of Canada from colony to nation. Visitors tour bedrooms, cooks' quarters, and study, all furnished to illustrate domestic life at the time of Macdonald's early career. Formal exhibit rooms chronicle the great man's career and cover the history of Bellevue itself, which was fashioned as an Italian villa. The extensive gardens are kept in condition by costumed gardeners using nineteenth-century methods. On returning to Kingston's historic downtown, you'll agree that the civic pride of Kingstonians is well founded.

Kingston Tourist Information Office
(613) 548-4415

Bellevue House
Daily 10:00-5:00
(613) 545-8666

WESTPORT
Silver White Winters

Evergreen boughs heavy-laden with fresh snow, a white-tailed deer poised motionless just ahead on the trail, cloudless skies and brilliant sunshine. Winter at Frontenac Provincial Park is a very special experience, as any skier, snowshoer or hiker will tell you with enthusiasm. Comprising 5,130 hectares, it is one of our largest provincial parks, and because of its status as a wilderness park its forests can be admired in their pristine condition.

From Kingston drive north on Highway 38 to County Road 5; head east to the village of Sydenham and then north on County Road 19. The route from there is well marked. From Ottawa, drive west along Highway 7 to Highway 38 and head south; follow 5 and 19 as above to Sydenham and the park. Before heading out for a winter wilderness adventure, be sure to check in at the entrance trail-centre for advice on routes, snow depth, lake-ice conditions and a weather forecast.

Those keen for a short but very sweet taste of Canadian winter will want to try out the 1.5-kilometre Arab Lake Gorge trail (interpretive brochure available). This easy but beautiful trail and boardwalk is most suitable for snowshoers and hikers, although if the snow is deep it may provide hikers with a little more exercise than they bargained for.

The trail curves through marshy beaver ponds embraced by high granite cliffs. Although the cliffs are too rugged for summertime hiking, winter voyageurs ascend and descend them over deep layers of snow and fallen trees. Frontenac can be magically empty, particularly on weekdays. The glittering snow is sculpted by the wind and engraved with countless tracks of mice, hare, birds and deer. What sounds there are—the tinkle of ice-encrusted twigs or the nasal call of a nuthatch—serve to heighten the sense of solitude. Perhaps this might be how Ontario appeared to early explorers and settlers. Frontenac is favoured by winter sports enthusiasts who thrill to exploring the

wilderness without being pampered. While ski-patrol volunteers traverse the park, leaving their trails for later skiers, none of the trails are groomed—and avid skiers love it that way. Many who visit the park specialize in "bushwhacking," or back-country skiing, rewarded by sights such as a wolf or a great horned owl. At its peak in February is ice fishing for splake, brook trout, perch, pike and crappie on several interior lakes. Since snowmobiles and cars are not allowed in the park, those determined to fish must pack their own gear and travel by ski or snowshoe.

Does Frontenac sound like too much of a wilderness trek for you? Never fear, the competent staff provide a full slate of weekend workshops to upgrade your skills. The topics include ski techniques, safety and waxing; ice fishing; showshoeing; winter camping (an increasingly popular pastime at Frontenac); winter photography and wilderness survival. There are children's workshops and school-holiday programs as well.

By the time the golden late-afternoon sun slants through the trees, casting long lines of shadow on the snow, your invigorated muscles and peace-filled soul will be ready to seek the cozy side of Canadian winter. Exit the park and drive north on County Road 19; where 19 curves west towards Verona, take the gravel road that borders the park towards Fermoy. Although a secondary country road, it is well ploughed in winter. Northern scenery of lake, granite and white pine is interrupted occasionally by a log house or farm wearing a thick comforter of snow. Upon reaching County Road 8, head east towards Westport.

Originally a lumber and railroad town, Westport now makes its living from boaters on the Rideau Canal during the summer and skiers during the winter. Relax over a meal (filling and bargain-priced) at the Cove, located where the main drag meets Upper Rideau Lake. For those with a mind to turn a

Cross-country skiing, Frontenac Provincial Park.

day into a weekend, the Cove's hospitality extends to rooms, and a session in the sauna or hot tub is a perfect complement to a stay in the fireplace suite.

Westport has several shops of interest. Try out Ingmar's (clothing), North of the Border, Brown Bear and the Village Green (paintings, sculpture, pottery and souvenirs) or Silver and Mask (art with a Latin American twist). When Sutherland's Scottish Bake Shop closes for part of the winter, try Chocolate Treats.

Almond buttercreams and peanut clusters: what a way to wrap up a winter's day!

If you thrill to silver white winters that melt into spring, Frontenac Provincial Park just might become one of your favourite things.

Frontenac Provincial Park
Open daily
(613) 376-3489

24

KINGSTON
Military Manoeuvres

Boom! The thunder of cannon fire echoes around the walled courtyard. "Forward march!" screams the drill sergeant, and dozens of cleated heels slap the pavement in unison. The evening sky is smudged with black smoke and lit by flashes of orange as the cannon is answered by a round of musket fire. Scenes of yesteryear? No, this is present-day Kingston, where the traditions of our military past are kept alive at Old Fort Henry, the Canadian Forces Communications and Electronics Museum and the Royal Military College Museum.

These three sites are located in close proximity to one another. Travel from downtown Kingston eastward along Highway 2 (refer to the map for trip 22). You can't miss the signs for Old Fort Henry. It's worth the drive up the long hill to the fort just to take in the sweeping view of the Royal Military College immediately below, Kingston's lovely waterfront in the middle distance and the islands of the St. Lawrence along the horizon.

From the replica nineteenth-century uniforms to the lilt of a fife carried on the breeze, the staff at the fort work hard to recreate military life in Upper Canada. Visitors may wander around with a guidebook or take in one of the tours offered throughout the day. The fort is a magnificent facility, complete with imposing ramparts, drawbridge, battery and parade grounds. The thick stone walls contain scores of rooms, many made up to look as they did in 1830s when the fort was the main military establishment in the colony. There are cells, kitchens, officers' quarters, a wine cellar, mess, barracks and powder magazine. Costumed interpreters detail military life, from the soldiers' regimen of tedious drills and corporeal punishment, to the harsh living conditions offered their families.

Several rooms are devoted to the evolution of military equipment and artillery, with a host of artifacts—field guns, ammunition, rifles— and explanatory text. The fort includes several shops selling reproduction housewares, clothing, artwork and books, all with a military theme. The Garrison Restaurant will fill the hunger gap during lunch hour.

A full slate of special events means that a Fort Henry visit may last an entire day. Pick up a copy of the Fort Henry Gazette for information on Victoria Day celebrations, vintage car shows, symphony concerts and Celtic Festivals. On a daily basis, there are children's military muster parades, schoolroom programs, puppet shows, pipe bands and the spectacular afternoon and evening drills. The world-famous sunset Ceremonial Retreat, held twice weekly during the summer, is a tribute to the era when the British redcoats acted as our main protectors. The Fort Henry Guard, with 141 members, puts on a display of music, cannon fire and mock battles guaranteed to send thrills down your spine. Afternoon drills are performed by a smaller unit, and they are also a wonderful history lesson, as the officer in charge narrates each manoeuvre, march and firing. Every movement is executed with...well...military precision.

For the true armed-forces devotee, there are two other Kingston sights worth noting. The Royal Military College Museum is on the RMC grounds, housed in a lakefront Martello Tower, the largest of these towers in the Kingston area. (The college campus itself, a collection of stately historic buildings just downhill from Fort Henry, is well worth a walking tour.) The tower was part of Fort Frederick, built to protect the Royal Dockyard located on the waterfront in this vicinity, and the museum displays some items from the fort.

Photographs, memoirs and text relate the story of the Royal Military College, the first military college in the Commonwealth to achieve university status. Displays also chronicle the careers of some of the college's most illustrious graduates. The second floor of the museum contains the Douglas small-arms collection, considered one of the best of its

The British Square, Old Fort Henry.

kind in North America, not only for its size and completeness, but also for the many unusual items in the collection.

Now it's back to the car to drive to the Canadian Forces Communications and Electronics Museum. Drive east on Highway 2 to the Kingston military base and follow signs to the museum, housed in the Vimy Barracks. Displays trace the development of communications within the military, highlighting the role of the Canadian Signal Corps, the oldest such unit in the Common-wealth. The story begins with lonely station operators on the frontier in the North West Territories and brings you up to the sophisticated modern technology of the Gulf War. Most enlightening are the mock-ups of communications rooms and field depots; these are effective illustrations of the step-by-step improvements in battlefield communications, from flag signals to high-tech computer systems. The museum includes a snack bar and gift shop.

It may be said that Ontario's beginnings are based in the military forts and outposts built along the Great Lakes. Take a day to appreciate our red coated history in its principal home, Kingston.

Old Fort Henry
Mid-May to mid-October:
Daily 10:00-5:00
(613) 542-7388

Royal Military College Museum
Mid-June to September:
Daily 10:00-5:00
(613) 541-6664

Canadian Forces
Communications and Electronics Museum
September to mid-May:
Monday-Friday 8:00-4:00
Mid-May to September:
Daily 10:00-4:00
(613) 541-5395

WOLFE ISLAND
Islands in the Stream

Oh, the magical allure of island life! Tranquility, self-reliance and a physical and social environment so compact that it allows for easy familiarity. Wolfe and Simcoe islands, just off Kingston's watery front porch, allow travellers to experience a day of island life.

While there are several inhabited islands in the Kingston area, and each has its own charm, Wolfe and Simcoe islands are most easily reached and offer the greatest diversity. Begin an island adventure by boarding the *Wolfe Islander III* at the docks in downtown Kingston (refer to the map for trip 22). Operating year-round, this free ferry with a capacity of 55 cars and 300 people takes 20 minutes to reach Wolfe Island. (Although ferries run very frequently, there can be a frustrating line-up on summer weekends; plan your trip accordingly.) You may want to join many others crossing the ferry with bicycles instead of cars, because Wolfe Island is beloved by cyclists for its flat topography and because it offers an appealing opportunity to bike to the United States and back in a day.

The ferry disembarks at Marysville, the only settlement on Wolfe Island. The main street is also Highway 96, and most of the crowd will head right, towards the Cape Vincent ferry to the United States. Leave the masses, and turn to the left at Highway 96. First things first: drop in at the Wolfe Island Bakery for some extraordinarily good, hot-from-the-oven cinnamon buns to enjoy at any of the scenic spots along the road. Then continue along the highway into the countryside.

One hundred years ago, Wolfe Island was a bustling community of farmers, millers, boat-builders and fishermen. The population declined dramatically early in this century, which means that the gravel roadways are uncrowded and the scenery remains like that of rural mainland Ontario about 50 years ago. There are kilometres of small farms, many with rugged stone farmhouses, verdant meadows dotted with apple blossoms in

spring and daisies in summer, and pebbled coves with bobbing sailboats and cormorants spreading their wings to dry.

The decline in prosperity means that Wolfe Island is a delight for photographers and naturalists. There are scores of abandoned farms, schools and churches, some in stone and many of timber, all worthy of a photograph. Large areas of pasture make the island good habitat for many species of field sparrows, hawks and owls, which in turn attract goodly numbers of birdwatchers.

A couple of kilometres out of Marysville you will pass a wet and reedy ditch, the remnants of a mid-nineteenth-century attempt to attract barge traffic. Continue eastward, and Highway 96 becomes a maple-lined gravel laneway with enough short, but steep, hills and sharp turns to make for enjoyable pleasure driving. Follow these twists to the Scotch Block's (the original name for this community) Christ Church, which has witnessed steady use since its beginnings in 1862.

After your fill of back-roading, retrace your route to Marysville. Its most famous business, the General Wolfe Hotel, has dispensed hospitality for over a century and has a wide reputation for good food. The pub/pool room serves generous portions of meat-and-potatoes cooking while the dining room serves up frogs' legs, island-raised pheasant and French pastries; both menus come at a fraction of the cost of those in city restaurants. Walk west along Main Street. Take an appreciative glance at the limestone town hall. Tucked away behind it is a minuscule white frame building, one of Ontario's smallest public libraries.

Return to the car and head into the countryside west of Marysville. The western part of the island is more hilly than the eastern end and the drive along the north shore has good vistas of distant Kingston and the pretty St. Lawrence islands. The southwest corner of the island is the Bear

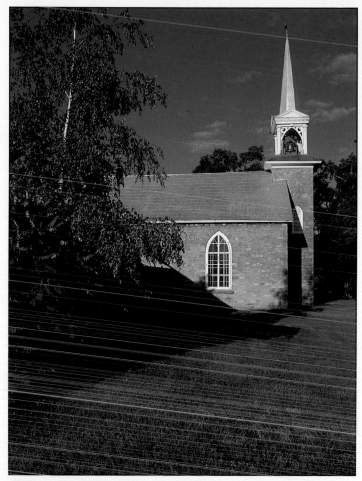

Trinity Church, Marysville, Wolfe Island.

Point Nature Preserve. Locals say that a good bathing beach can be reached via a lengthy hike through the preserve to the lake.

The northwestern corner of Wolfe Island, about 4 kilometres from Marysville, is where you'll find the ferry for Simcoe Island, which is much smaller and less developed than Wolfe Island. A visit here is sure to make you feel like a modern-day explorer. The ferry, Ontario's smallest with a capacity of two cars, operates when there is a car waiting at the dock. There is not much to do on Simcoe Island but take a walk. At the end of the gravel track (there is only one and it leads west from the ferry) is the island lighthouse. At some point you must rejoin civilization, so head back to Wolfe Island and board the *Wolfe Islander III* for the mainland.

The day has one more point of interest, Garden Island. Although the island no longer has ferry service, it is in plain view of ferry passengers, just northwest of Wolfe Island. Garden Island was an important ship-building community during the nineteenth century, and is now Ontario's best preserved "ghost town."

Wolfe Island is a refreshingly quiet oasis, caressed by river breezes and sweetened by summer sun. A leisurely exploration of its byways is a treat for those yearning to sample island life.

Wolfe Island Ferry
Schedule information
(613) 544-2231

General Wolfe Hotel
(613) 385-2611

26

LANARK
A Real Good Yarn

Ontario has its own mighty Mississippi River, and its power was harnessed to make Lanark County the engine of a vigorous textile industry. Although mills and textile factories were an important source of employment and commerce for over 150 years, the last one closed in 1989. The industry leaves behind a legacy of charming towns and factory-outlet shopping guaranteed to make a good trip.

Begin in Almonte (called "Little Manchester" because the majority of mills were here), northwest of Ottawa at the intersection of Highways 15 and 44. The river drops 20 metres in the course of its run through town, and it was this power potential that attracted mill owners during the mid-nineteenth century. There are good views of the many remaining mills from riverside parks throughout Almonte.

The Mississippi Valley Textile Museum is located at the heart of a handsome stone industrial complex at 3 Rosamond Street. Main floor mill offices with high tin ceilings, lovely hardwood floors and wainscotting now house exhibits on the valley textile industry. The building's top floor, originally used to store raw wool and finished goods (it still smells very much like sheep!), displays historic and contemporary looms. True to its roots, the valley has an active spinning and weaving guild and its handiwork is available at the museum's craft shop.

Almonte Town Hall

Drive to Almonte's downtown where there are several interesting craft and gift shops, among them, popular Peterson's Dairy Bar, and the Wool Palette, which stocks supplies for home crafters.

Leave Almonte by heading west on Main Street, and follow the signs out of town to the Mill of Kintail, a four-storey 1830s grist mill. This was the summer home and studio of Robert Tait Mackenzie. An attractive museum in a forest overlooking the Indian River chronicles Tait's fascinating career as military doctor, physical-education specialist and artist. The second story displays some of his fine works. From the mill, drive due south (*not* back through Almonte) and end up in Carleton Place.

There are three stops for those interested in textiles here. The first is the Mississippi Black Sheep Gallery, which is located at the corner of Bell and Bridge street and offers a friendly welcome to visitors. From floor to ceiling, it is a celebration of colour in cotton, woollen and blended yarns for spinning, weaving, and knitting. There is also an excellent supply of books on textiles.

Just around the corner on Bell Street, in a restored tannery, is the Leather Works Restaurant. Meals are served beneath rough beams and historic photographs of Carleton Place. The view of the river is wonderful, especially in springtime when the water level is just centimetres below the outdoor deck.

The centre of the Canadian sheep industry is the Canada Wool Growers Co operative on Franktown Road (Highway 15 at the south end of town), where a million kilograms of wool are graded annually. Phone ahead for weekday tours of the wool-grading process and visit the shop for high-quality woollen and sheepskin goods.

From Carleton Place, drive west on Highway 7, County Road 15 and then County Road 12 to tiny but busy Lanark. What a delightful find for shoppers! The Glenayr Kitten company has not one, but four, factory outlets here. Each one is different. There are lots of ladies' clothes, especially the quality knit coordinates that made Kitten's reputation, but also lingerie, men's wear, kid's clothing and shoes, and a plethora of costume jewellery. All are bargain priced. D & B Discount Shoestore is the place to visit for high-quality footwear at great prices. Lanark

has many, many other clothing and craft stores and eateries to visit—plan on at least a half-day to see them all.

Perth (via Highway 511) is the last town on the woollen trail. (En route you will pass Balderson Cheese, one of the few remaining dairy plants in the region. The store is a cornucopia of gourmet foods and specialty cheeses.) Perth's main draw for today is the Code Felt Mill on Herriott (just off Gore). The Code mill was built in 1876 to produce heavy socks for the North West Mounted Police. The outlet shop is a treasure trove of felt in 74 brilliant colours; by the piece or by the pound, it is remarkably inexpensive. There are also good quality blankets, linens, yarns and ribbons, and those felt boot-liners that many Canadians swear by for winter warmth.

The Mill Store at the corner of Foster and Gore in downtown Perth also draws bargain hunters. It carries clothing for the whole family, including wool sweaters, at good prices. If it is time for a meal, Perth is very accommodating, with several good eateries (see trip 28).

This adventure has been devoted to textiles, from picturesque mill towns to factory-outlet shopping. The day will make a good yarn for all travellers.

Mississippi Valley Textile Museum
May-October:
Tuesday-Friday 10:00-4:00
Saturday 10:00-5:00
Sunday 1:00-5:00
(613) 256-3754

The Mill of Kintail
Mid-May to September:
Daily 10:00-5:00
September to mid-October:
Wednesday-Sunday 10:30-4:30
Weekends and holidays 10:00-4:30
(613) 256-3610

Canadian Wool Growers
(613) 257-2714

Most shops open standard business hours

27

PAKENHAM
Maples and Moguls

While maple syrup celebrations mark the commencement of spring in some regions of the province, in other regions spring means skiing in brilliant sunshine and balmy temperatures. Eastern Ontario is doubly fortunate in having a climate that allows for both late-season skiing and early-season maple syrup at the same time. Visit Fulton's Pancake House and Mount Pakenham Ski Resort (both near Almonte) in order to usher out winter and welcome in spring with style.

Lanark County is self-titled the Maple Syrup Capital of Ontario, and Fulton's Pancake House is one of many establishments catering to pancake and syrup aficionados. Fulton's is particularly recommended because it operates year-round, and, besides the traditional pancake house, it offers a comprehensive program of activities related to the sugar bush. From Almonte, drive north on Highway 15. Turn west at Cedar Hill Road and follow signs to Fulton's.

Catch the spirit of maple-syrup season in the pancake house, where families from town and country sit along picnic tables to feast on mountains of pancakes, sausage and syrup, as well as maple-baked beans, maple apple pie and maple cheesecake. Fulton's is always busy, but never too crowded, and the friendly atmosphere is a reminder that rural Ontarians have been offering springtime syrup and hospitality to visitors for over a century.

After a filling repast, a hike along Fulton's three trails (total 12 kilometres) is just the thing. They are colour-coded for distance and are sign-posted with information on the sugar bush. (During winter these trails are groomed for cross-country skiing and free baby-sitting is offered to skiers on Sundays.) You'll gain an appreciation of the scale of Fulton's operation by observing the kilometres of pipeline used to carry sap from 6,000 taps to the evaporator.

The children's playground is always a popular place, as is the sugar shack, where staff explain traditional and modern methods of syrup production. Fulton family members carry on both techniques, each year hand-carrying 150 buckets of sap to an old-fashioned wood-fired evaporator in remembrance of John Fulton, who first made syrup on this farm in the 1840s.

Fulton's offers a congenial welcome year-round to groups and individuals looking for a country outing. The trails and gift shop are open, and family gatherings and tour groups are given a country dinner and music. Special events include Easter-egg hunts, sleigh and wagon rides, fall corn roasts, and photography and naturalist workshops.

Drive back to Highway 15 and head north to Pakenham. This village is known for two features. It has North America's only five-span stone bridge. During spring run-off the Mississippi River provides a spectacular show of white-water sound and fury as it churns under the bridge. There is a good observation point in Pakenham Bridge Conservation Area.

Pakenham's second focal point is the Pakenham General Store, billed as Canada's oldest original country store. A plaque near the front door lists all proprietors, with the Scotts and Browns in continuous ownership for 150 years. This amiable spot serves home baking, ice cream and dry goods, in addition to local pottery, jewellery, moccasins and books. Other shopping places in and around Pakenham include Paddye Mann Designs (ladies' clothing), Stonebridge Heirlooms (antiques, especially housewares), Lois' Woolen Workshop (parka-making supplies), and Toby's Studio (folk art). Ask at the general store for a map of local shops and studios.

It's time to wear off the calories gained at Fulton's. From Pakenham head south on Highway 15 to McWatty Road and follow signs to Mount Pakenham Ski Resort, advertised as Eastern Ontario's most complete alpine and cross-country centre. Excellent

Pakenham Bridge, Mississippi River.

snow-making and grooming facilities mean a long season, usually stretching from early December until early April. And now for the vital statistics: there are eight downhill runs, a vertical drop of 90 metres, plenty of lifts (a quad, a double, T-bars and rope tows), lighting for night skiing and a variety of membership and lift packages.

For wilderness skiing buffs there are 35 kilometres of cross-country trails, groomed and set, including a 1-kilometre run that is lit for night-time enjoyment. As with alpine skiing, there are rentals and a full slate of lessons. Special events are run several times a season. Christmas and March school holidays are busy times at Mount Pakenham, when 135 instructors lead children's camps. Mount Pakenham staff are very experienced with kids, since about 500 children visit each weekday for school-sponsored outings. Last,

but not least, facilities include a cafeteria, bar and lounge.

Bidding adieu to winter and bienvenue to spring can be accomplished in one day in northern Lanark County, land of maples and moguls.

Fulton's Pancake House
March & April:
Daily 9:00-5:00
Summer and fall:
Phone for times
Winter:
Saturday & Sunday 10:00-4:00
otherwise, by appointment
(613) 256-3867

Mount Pakenham ski lodge:
(613) 624-5290

28

PERTH
Written in Stone

Perth may be Ontario's most picturesque town. Its main streets are straight lines of classic commercial blocks built over a century ago. This architectural heritage, an historic inn and several excellent restaurants make Perth the choice of discriminating daytrippers.

Perth was settled by Scots immigrants, many of them discharged officers from the War of 1812. They brought money and managerial expertise to found a prosperous business community based on lumber and grain milling, whisky and woollens. Stonemasons who laboured on the Rideau Canal used their considerable construction skills to create a town rich in limestone and sandstone buildings.

A historic walking tour begins at Gore and Market Square in front of impressive Town Hall, constructed from local sandstone. Town Hall was built in 1863 and has served as council quarters and concert hall. Kitty-corner is the remarkable McMillan Building (1907), originally a Carnegie Library and designed as a facsimile of the Bank of Montreal building in Toronto. River Guild at 51 Gore East sells a diverse range of crafts, from fine batiks of local scenes to sheepskin clothing to pottery and blown glass. Next door is Valley Books, a great browse.

Imposing Matheson House (11 Gore Street East) was originally constructed as the home of a judge and senator, and is now the Perth Museum. Two floors of displays cover local history from Woodland Indians through to early farming and businesses. There are several rooms restored to illustrate the life in a well-to-do family of the mid-1800s. The museum's most notorious artifacts are the pistols used in Canada's last duel, fought between articling law students over a local governess (1833). The garden is restored to the 1840s period and is a lovely respite from main street bustle.

Nearby Matheson House is Shaw's, Perth's most respected clothing store, operated by the family since 1858. Backtrack a little to Herriott Street and turn right. Number 50 is a regal, red sandstone house built for the Code family, who ran the family felt mill across the street in the 1870s. You can take a pleasant stroll in Code and Stewart parks which sit on opposite banks of the river; there is a pretty waterfall and a pedestrian bridge.

Return to Gore Street. The walk may have stimulated the appetite, so it's a good thing that there are several restaurants to choose from. "At E's" is well recommended, as is the Maximilian Dining Lounge. The former specializes in homemade pasta and chicken dishes. (Do not miss exquisite raspberry-chocolate bash or equally good peanut-butter pie). Maximilian offers huge servings of schnitzel, goulash and other German fare; service and food are first rate. Light meals and good sweets (almond-maple cheesecake and rhubarb sour-cream pie) are available at the Courtyard Tea Room. All three establishments overlook the turning basin of the Tay Canal and are located in commercial blocks dating to the nineteenth century.

Head southeast along Gore to Harvey Street and McMartin House (1830). In a town of prominent lawyers, this was the home of Perth's first. Typical of the Federal style popular in the eastern United States, McMartin House features a symmetrical facade, contrasting marblework, and an elliptical fanlight over the entrance. The most distinguishing feature is an extravagant widow's walk with flanking lanterns.

Inge-Va is a captivating, romantic dwelling located at the corner of Craig and Wilson (walk along Gore to Craig, turn right, and it is a short block along). An excellent example of Georgian neo-classical design, Inge-Va was the home of Reverend Harris of the Perth military settlement. This stone home has a delicate and lacy transom and sidelights, multi-paned windows and a pretty rose garden.

Retrace your steps along Craig, crossing Gore to reach Drummond, a good point from

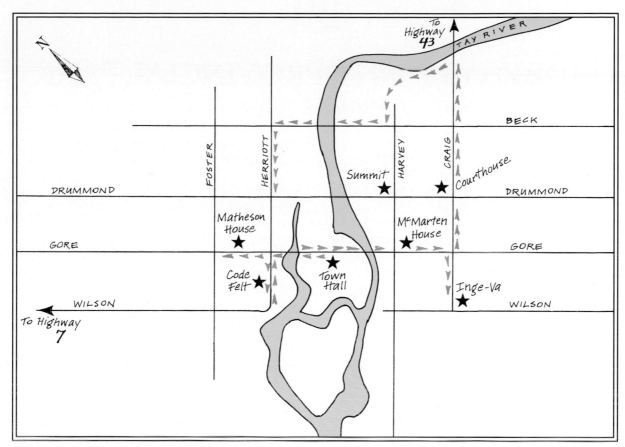

Perth

which to admire the 1842 Courthouse and County Gaol (located just behind). A block further along, at Harvey and Drummond, is Summit House, which dates to the 1820s. Torontonians will recognize this as a replica of "The Grange," and like the Grange, this is one of Ontario's first houses built of brick.

Devotees of heritage inns will eagerly anticipate the walk further along to 23 Drummond, the Perth Manor, known for fine dining and accommodations. This 1878 Italianate villa was home to a cabinet minister and is graced by elegant fireplaces, bay windows and period decorations. The food earns praise from reviewers and the expansive gardens make for a very pleasant stop.

Walk northeast along Craig Street. Where Craig crosses the Tay Canal is the vicinity of the famous last duel. The canal was built during the 1830s to link Perth with the Rideau Canal and bring commercial and industrial prosperity to town. Indeed, the

turning basin in downtown Perth was surrounded with warehouses built to receive and send goods from distant ports. Passenger steamers also plied the canal. Today the canal brings recreational boaters from the Rideau Waterway into downtown Perth. The canal towpath makes for a leisurely summertime stroll.

Return to downtown via Herriott Street. The Old Firehall on Herriott between Drummond and Gore dates to 1855; today it is an art gallery featuring Lanark County painting, weaving, pottery and other crafts.

Perth is a happy marriage of prosperity and Victorian elegance. It will be a favourite destination for years to come.

Perth Museum
Monday-Saturday 10:00-5:00
Sunday 1:00-4:00
(613) 267-1947

29

MURPHYS POINT PROVINCIAL PARK
Mine, All Mine

The rock next to your hand glistens with moisture, and in the dim light its face gleams in unworldly shades of silver, amber, pink and green. Watch out! Duck your head to narrowly miss banging your hardhat on a mine timber. Step into a spacious cavern where light pours in from an overhead opening framed with ferns and moss. Drill bits poke through the rock, left to rust by the previous workers.

It may sound like stepping into an adventure novel, but you are actually enjoying a visit to Murphys Point Provincial Park. The park is 1,240 hectares of forest and lakeshore along Big Rideau Lake south of Perth. Those who haven't visited an Ontario provincial park for some time may be surprised at the extensive

visitor programs and improved facilities that make our parks super daytrip destinations.

Murphys Point is located on the Frontenac Axis, a spur of rocky Canadian shield that pokes southward towards Kingston. Much of the visitor activity focuses on the "point" area of the park that juts out into Big Rideau Lake. The forest is primarily deciduous and is so dense with saplings that it appears fresh and green all summer long. Stout white birch brighten the scene during the day and are ghostly beautiful after dark. Small mammals and birds abound, and the occasional white-tail deer may pose long enough for a photograph. Black Creek flows through aspen wetland and beaver ponds before emptying into Hogg Bay.

Silver Queen Mine, Murphys Point Provincial Park.

The park has a varied collection of hiking trails. Each trail is well maintained and signed. The Rocky Narrows Trail (2 kilometres) will lead you to a sandy beach for a quiet swim away from it all. The McParlan Trail (2.5 kilometres) travels along Hogg Bay to the mouth of Black Creek and the ruins of the 1810 Burgess Sawmill. The Sylvan Trail (2.5 kilometres) is a pleasant tour through mixed forest. The Point Trail (4 kilometres) connects with Sylvan and Rocky Narrows, and is a complete tour of the peninsula known as Murphys Point. The rugged Rideau Trail that travels from Kingston to Ottawa passes through the park for 6.5 kilometres. It is well marked, but is not an easy hike and is often wet; ask for advice at the park office.

The most interesting hike is along the Silver Queen Mine Trail. Park staff take guided tours of this very special 2-kilometre trail two or three times weekly during the summer, so be sure to phone ahead to confirm times and book a spot. During the first two decades of this century mining companies extracted mica, apatite, and feldspar from this area, shipping it from Hogg Bay along the Rideau Canal.

The initial portion of the trail, an old mining road, has stopping points with signs describing the mica-mining industry. Guides add information about some of the more intriguing inhabitants of Murphys Point such as monarch butterflies and black rat snakes. At the mine entrance, visitors don adjustable hardhats before descending the slippery rocks into the mine. A chart indicates that the rock here is extremely old, formed about one billion years ago. As that molten rock cooled, minerals formed in pockets, to be exposed through upheaval, glaciation and erosion.

The rock face sparkles with silvery mica, as does much of the ground in the vicinity. (Do not pick your own sample; there are free samples available at the end of the tour.) Silver Queen's mica has "perfect cleavage,"

meaning that it easily sheets into pieces 1/1000 of an inch thick. These sheets were "cobbed" (broken into evenly-sized pieces) at a nearby shed and sold for use as electrical insulation and lamp glass. Apatite was also mined for use as a fertilizer; its effectiveness is seen at the mine, where ferns and mosses grow profusely over patches of apatite near the surface. Feldspar was used as a glazing in the ceramics industry.

A miner's life was not an enviable one. For a mighty 70 cents a day, he worked at digging through the rock with hand-pick and sledge-hammer. Black-powder explosions added an element of danger. The bunkhouse is on the tour. Up to 22 men ate and slept here for nine months a year (the other three months would be spent farming). The bunkhouse rules: no drinking, no gambling, no talking at the table. These were implemented in an effort to reduce the injury-producing arguments that hamper mine production.

After a walk to the Silver Queen Mine, there are many other activities to fill a day at Murphys Point. There are two sandy beaches where the shallow water warms to a pleasant temperature. There are plenty of picnic tables and barbecues, and the main beach has a children's play area. Fisherfolk may try for bass, pike and lake trout. Park staff run a terrific program of special events throughout the summer, such as nature walks, canoe hikes, children's games and craft activities, films and lectures. On some very special evenings, "spirit walks" go to the mine after dark. A costumed character, Mica Mike, often appears on these walks and at campfire singsongs.

Murphys Point: a gem of a daytrip!

Murphys Point Provincial Park
Mine tours conducted June to September
(613) 267-5060

Along the Thousand Islands Parkway west of Brockville.

30

ROCKPORT
Miles of Isles

Imagine yourself in a land of enchantment: glittering waters spotted with countless rocky islets, some large enough to support turreted castles, most so tiny that only a few windswept pines soften their shores; sailboats and cruisers, some bearing the insignia of distant nations, darting merrily across an international boundary; a shoreline mosaic of Victorian summer homes and quiet villages. Live out that dream along the stretch of the St. Lawrence River between Gananoque and Brockville known as the Thousand Islands.

The Thousand Islands Parkway is a scenic shoreline drive connecting these two towns. Begin an island day at Brockville, heading west along the Parkway, ending up in Gananoque. (A very pleasant alternative is to park the car and make use of the bike path which runs alongside the roadway.) Maps are available at the parkway entrance.

The shoreline is managed by the St. Lawrence Parks Commission, which has done an excellent job of providing roadside parks for swimming and boating. Perhaps the most rewarding park along the river is at Brown's Bay—especially for those smart enough to bring along a picnic. Young and old appreciate the warm waters of the beach, the grand view of the river and the fascinating historic display. It includes the remains of a gunboat found in local waters and other artifacts from the war of 1812. Perched atop a pink granite outcrop is a small building with exhibits on the natural beauty of the islands that emphasize the river as habitat, water source and transportation route.

Brown's Bay is the point of departure for the privately run Grenadier Island ferry service. The boat (circa 1929) departs several times daily and the island, part of St. Lawrence Islands National Park, provides hiking trails and camp sites.

Mallorytown Landing is the focus of many of the interpretive programs offered by St.

Lawrence Islands National Park, including films, games and lectures. Visitors camping on islands participate through the "floating interpretation centre" run by park staff.

Continuing westward, the next stop is tiny Rockport, established as a Loyalist settlement during Ontario's early years. Although contemporary Rockport caters to boaters and daytrippers, the village originally had a cheese factory and several stores and inns. The Andress Boatworks remains from the early days, and fortunate visitors may catch a glimpse of boat builders repairing a beautiful antique craft.

A cruise with Rockport Boat Lines is a good way to make the most of a Thousand Islands day. Because Rockport is in the heart of the islands, no time is spent travelling between the dock and pleasant scenery. The captain, a seasoned veteran of the river, narrates the one-hour cruise and charts a course with plenty of fodder for the shutterbug.

The Zavikon Islands are first on the agenda. A large white house sits on one island in Canadian waters, while its flagpole on a nearby islet sits in American waters. The connecting bridge—less than 10 metres long—is thus the shortest international bridge in the world. Among the other islands included in the itinerary is Deer Island, named for its winter deer population but more notorious for its summertime nudists (they belong to a Yale University fraternity).

Cruisers are taken through the stretch of river known as Millionaires' Row. Whether they are called mansions or summer homes, these places make for wonderful viewing and the list of owners reads like a who's who: Helena Rubenstein, Arthur Godfrey, and the Pullman family, for starters. Not all Thousand Island cottages are grand affairs; many, especially those on the Canadian side, are simple A-frames situated on islands just a bit larger in area than the cottage. Between marvelling at

The shortest international bridge, Zavikon Islands.

the islands, listening to the captain's stories of pirates and smugglers, and watching the passing yachts, there's never a dull moment on the river.

On the return trip to Rockport, catch the view of St. Brendan's Church, its clapboard weathered by over a century of winters, poised on the rocks high above the village. St. Brendan is the patron saint of mariners and a service is held each spring in which the congregation gathers on the river, in boats large and small, to be blessed for the coming season.

Visit the Ship's Galley in Rockport for seafood, steak and chicken. You may be in time for the Sunday champagne brunch, Wednesday's codtail dinner or Friday's buffet. Otherwise, return to the car and continue along the parkway.

The next village in a westward tour is Ivy Lea, famous both for its century-old summer homes and the graceful international bridge

that traverses the river. Visitors may ascend the 120-metre Skydeck (via high-speed elevators) for an eagle's-eye look at the region. Ivy Lea boat tours provide an hour-and-a-half cruise aboard a reproduction paddlewheeler. The boat is small enough that it can explore some tight island passages larger vessels cannot manage. Summer tours include a stop at Boldt Castle on Heart Island, a 120-room reproduction of an European castle built by George Boldt (owner of the Waldorf Astoria hotel) for his wife, Louise. Her untimely death halted construction and modern-day visitors tour the romantic unfinished castle and grounds. Boldt Castle is actually in the United States, so proper identification is required.

The last two riverside stopping points are Landons Bay (popular with anglers trying for the legendary St. Lawrence bass, pike and muskie) and Gray's Beach (a good spot for a swim).

Gananoque is the western finale to the parkway and offers the tourist a diverse range of attractions. In the north end of town you can visit the 1000 Islands Wild Kingdom, a 50-acre private zoo. Gananoque's main street (King) includes the Gan Mill Outlet for family clothing and the Gananoque Shoe Outlet for men's and women's shoes; both have discount prices. At the corner of King and Factory Lane (at the eastern end of downtown) is the Gananoque Museum. Furniture, clothing, photographs, antique St. Lawrence decoys and an impressive collection of dolls highlight the collection representing Gananoque over the past two centuries.

Gananoque has more restaurants than any other town of its size. Located just south of the museum, the Golden Apple has served fine food since 1928. The garden patio is a charming setting for lunch, which may include pasta, sandwiches and lovely homemade soups; the house specialty, roast beef, is the mainstay of the dinner menu. A little further east on King Street (number 250) is the justifiably famous Athlone Inn. In a very elegant setting, European cuisine is prepared and served with style (dinner only, reservations advised). The Britton House bed-and-breakfast is a turn-of-the-century home located near the harbour; it includes a restaurant called Cook Not Mad. The prix-fixe menu emphasizes locally grown foods such as trout and lamb, vegetables from the home garden and seasonal desserts (dinner only).

The harbour is busy all summer long with passengers enjoying the Gananoque Boat Line's one- and three-hour long tours of the Thousand Islands. These triple-decker boats are equipped with licensed snack bars and washrooms. The longer cruise stops at Boldt Castle.

A choice place to cool off on a warm summer evening is the Thousands Islands Playhouse located in Gananoque's refurbished canoe club. Musicals, drama and light summer comedy fill out a season that delights over 30,000 theatregoers each summer.

One trip is not enough to fully savour the unique beauty of the region originally called the "Garden of the Great Spirit," and you will leave promising to return.

Rockport Boat Lines
Mid-April to November
1-800-563-TOUR

Ivy Lea Boat Tours
Mid-May to mid-October
(613) 659-2293

1000 Islands Wild Kingdom
Daily 9:00-5:00
(613) 382-7141

Gananoque Boat Line
Mid-May to October
(613) 382-2144

Gananoque Museum
Mid-May to mid-October:
Monday-Friday 10:00-5:00
July & August:
Monday-Friday 10:00-8:00
Saturday 10:00-5:00 Sunday 12:00-5:00
(613) 382-4024

31

ATHENS
Painting the Town Red

Athens is one small town determined to carve a large niche for itself in the affections of daytrippers. Athens is about 22 kilometres northwest of Brockville along Highways 29 and 42. Athens was the first community in Ontario to paint itself red—well, a lot of different colours really—by commissioning professional artists to paint murals on the walls of businesses and civic buildings.

Pick up a walking tour of the murals at the town hall on the main street and wander the streets, pausing to admire your particular favourites. It might be a scene of small-town life in a gentler age, such as "The Gathering," which depicts several old-timers having a chin-wag around the stove in the general store, or peaceful "Picnic Scene, Charleston Lake," a 1912 outing at a nearby lake. Whatever your favourite, be sure to include "Athens High School Graduation, 1921" in your tour, because it features a nifty optical illusion. There is a Model-T depicted in the painting, and if you drive by slowly the car appears to be facing you, regardless of your position.

Not only is Athens worthy of a visit because of its murals, but it is the convenient starting point for a tour of the region, which abounds in antique shops. From Athens, drive south towards Charleston Lake Provincial Park. About 7 kilometres out of town pull into Restoration Farm Antiques. This is the Cadillac of antique stores. Pre-Confederation Canadian furniture, artwork and household effects are cleverly displayed in a 1845 stone farmhouse. Victorian linens spill out of dresser drawers, an ancient man's shaving kit is in the bathroom, and primitive wooden bowls and blackened pots sit on a rustic hearth.

The scene at Restoration Farm is so stunningly effective that you will not want to pull yourself away, but away you must. Return to Athens and head west along Highway 42. The next village is Delta. The main sight here is the 1810 Delta Old Mill,

with two floors of interesting exhibits on local history and mill technology.

Further west Highway 42 meets Highway 15, where you will head north to Crosby. Just west of Highway 15 in Crosby is Crosby Painter's Corner. The speciality here is china, porcelain and glass. This small shop carries an excellent selection of cranberry glass, and china from makers such as Wedgwood, Royal Nippon, and Ridgway. Some of these items date to before 1850. There are also historic prints of the region.

Return to Highway 15 and drive north to pretty Portland and two charming eateries. High on a hill on the way into town is the Portland School House (1888), a square, red-brick schoolhouse turned restaurant. The atmosphere is very authentic, with antique desks for children to sit at, original texts and maps on the walls, and the menu neatly scripted on the blackboard. A delightful place for a sandwich or snack.

Head off the highway to Portland's waterfront and grand Gallagher House. The main building was built almost a century ago by businessman Albert Gallagher, who ran a shipping line on the Rideau Canal. The hospitality at Gallagher is gracious and the food very good. There is always a good selection of homemade soups and sandwiches at lunch (the specialty is Irish Stone Soup), and a choice of chicken, fish, pasta or beef at dinner. The desserts range from fresh berry crisp to Schnapps sundaes.

Well-laden for the remainder of the antique tour, continue north on Highway 15 and head west on County Road 1 to Rideau Ferry. Several kilometres along is legendary Rideau Antiques. An abbreviated list of what may be found includes bird cages, crocks, windows, doors, plant pots, candlesticks, needlework, transformers, milk cans, wire fences, street signs and antique tools. And that's just the front yard!

Rideau Antiques

Several inside rooms hold stacks upon stacks of silver flatware, china, sausage stuffers, cameras, clocks, historic photographs. Don't worry about being a bull in a china shop—it looks as if the bull has already been here. Wade through the backyard to find piles of furniture parts—legs, arms, headboards, side rails, drawers. If you are missing a bit of china or a dresser doorknob for a prized set, come to Rideau Antiques.

Just a little further west of Rideau Antiques is Glenburnie Antiques. Take a breath and prepare for a drastic change of pace. Glenburnie's specialty is very fine eighteenth- and nineteenth-century furniture and objets

d'art, for example, a William IV sofa (1825) or an Edwardian silverplate fish-serving dish. An elegant way to end the day.

Delta Old Mill
Mid-May to September:
Daily 10:00-5:00
September to mid-October:
Saturday and Sunday: 10:00-5:00
(613) 928-2658

Most stores and restaurants open standard business hours

Merrickville Blockhouse

32

MERRICKVILLE

By's Byway North

The Rideau Canal is a national treasure. Running between Kingston and Ottawa, it links two rivers and numerous lakes in a world-class recreational boatway. There is much to see along the Rideau, so it is described in two daytrips, one covering Ottawa to Smiths Falls, and one covering Smiths Falls to Kingston.

Today's trip starts as lock-builder Colonel John By did, at the site of the Ottawa locks, hidden deep in the valley between the Château Laurier and Parliament Hill. Summertime visitors hover canal-side to scrutinize luxurious yachts navigating the eight steep locks. The locks are fashioned from limestone quarried from these very cliffs. For those who are enticed by the boating life, narrated boat tours depart from behind the National Arts Centre for Dow's Lake (the centre is across Wellington).

Beside the locks stands By's commissariat (treasury), Ottawa's oldest stone building. It is now the Bytown Museum, featuring displays on local history and a portrayal of By's career. He was renowned as an engineering genius who established a uniquely Canadian engineering tradition, adapting European construction methods to suit Canada's difficult climate and topography. Colonel By also coped with labour disputes and a complete lack of supporting transportation or local industry. Although he became a Canadian hero, By's career ended in failure in Britain because canal-building costs exceeded estimates. The museum also deals with the immigrant labourers who worked 16-hour days with hand tools to cut this 200-kilometre swath through bedrock, swamp and forest (circa 1830). Thousands died due to inadequate living conditions, malaria, bitter winters, mud slides and accidental explosions.

From the Ottawa Locks drive to Hog's Back Falls by way of Wellington and Colonel By Drive (a romantic drive when the canal is lit by globe lights and Parliament is silhouetted against the evening sky). All the water of the Rideau River thunders through the narrow rock chasm at Hog's Back with a force that tosses massive boulders like pebbles. The falls are wildly attractive, although By and his workers could hardly have seen them that way, since they were foiled here in several attempts at dam building. The story of their triumph is told on storyboards surrounding the falls—they highlight the canal as one of the greatest engineering feats of the nineteenth century. Hog's Back is the point of departure for trips upstream to Black's Rapids aboard the vintage steamboat *Bytown Pumper* (Sundays only).

Travel south along Highway 16, exiting the main road for Manotick. Head for five-storey Watson's Mill. This outstanding historic site is in working order and the flour ground each Wednesday (1 PM sharp) is offered for sale. The mill is also open for guided or self-guiding tours. Walk behind the mill and across the tiny footbridge to take the best photographs.

Manotick is a good stroll for shoppers, with a host of casual clothing stores, A Child's Garden (educational toys), A World of Dolls (a shop with a wide reputation), Cobblestones by the Mill (pottery supplies, ceramics and stoneware), the Weaver's House (pottery, table linens and other decorative ware) and European Antiques (eighteenth- and nineteenth-century furniture and objets d'art).

From Manotick, continue upstream along County Roads 13 and 2 to quaint Burritts Rapids, a model 1800s mill town. Those willing to wander the side streets are rewarded with scenes largely unchanged in decades: the houses are close together and range from simple clapboard to elaborate Victorian; two beautiful churches date back at least 130 years; the sense of peace is palpable. Burritts Rapids is also a good place to watch the locks in operation. In order to preserve the historic integrity of the canal, lock operators along the canal open and close the

Heritage House Museum, Smiths Falls.

huge oaken gates by hand-winch, as they have for over 160 years.

Merrickville, the next stop along the canal, is a delightful village sure to capture the hearts of travellers. The Merrickville Blockhouse, with metre-thick stone walls, is the second largest remaining blockhouse in Canada, and was constructed as part of a canal defense system. The blockhouse contains two floors of agricultural and domestic artifacts and displays on the typical life of a military officer and his family.

From the blockhouse, walk over the bridge to the Merrickville Industrial Ruins on Pig Island, which once bustled with 58 different enterprises, among them a foundry, tannery, cooper and several mills. The poignant ruins and the explanatory text make for an interesting visit.

Merrickville's great popularity with daytrippers is due in part to the diversity and

quality of its shops. A small sample includes the following: Village Metalsmiths has custom cast-metal signs and Victorian reproductions. Sinaao sells Arctic foods and crafts, including caribou steaks, wolfskin mukluks and wall hangings. Vintage clothing, from charming Victorian nightdresses to outrageous ladies' hats, is available at Now and Then Antiques. Waterways offers everything for the birdbrain, such as feeders, decoys, and field guides. Mirick's Landing Country Store is a diverse shop with folk art, souvenir clothing, stationery and books. The Hot Glass Studio (a few blocks from the river on Bruce Street) is where minerals and sand are turned into luminous beauty.

Merrickville is also popular because of its fine restaurants. Sir Sam Jakes' Inn serves meals in a floral dining room or a garden patio, with specialties such as Colonel By's Regimental Dinner for Two (just let's say it involves chicken, steak and shrimp). At the very hub of town is the Baldachin Restaurant with exceptional continental cookery, from flambées to seafood. Those with a sweet tooth will head for the Around the Corner Bakery, with almond cream horns and butter tarts at terrific prices.

Continue along the north side of the waterway (Highway 43). As you near Smiths Falls follow signs to the Heritage House Museum and Old Sly's Locks. Heritage House is a Victorian mansion dating to the 1860s, where seven fully furnished rooms, historic exhibits and special events present a lovely picture of life on the riverside, and rate a visit.

Now return north to Highway 43 and turn east (right). Make a left turn at Hershey Drive; follow the delectable scent to the factory with the huge Hersheybar on the front. Chocoholics beware! This is one dangerous place. There are self-guided tours overlooking the production floor. Drool longingly over huge vats of creamy chocolate being readied for the bar-moulding room; follow the goo as it is transformed into your favourite bar or treat, and then sent on to the wrapping room. Best (or perhaps worst) of all, the plant has a shop brimming with chocolate products, from gigantic bars to miniatures perfect for Hallowe'en treats, packaged or in bulk. All merchandise is at tremendous savings. Hershey's may not have much to do with the canal, but it is the sweetest way to wrap up a daytrip and is a sure winner with children.

If the canal captivates you, stay on in Smiths Falls for a second day, or save the treat of Rideau Canal South for another time.

Bytown Museum and Commissariat
April to November:
Monday-Saturday 10:00-4:00
Sunday 2:00-5:00
Closed Tuesday
(613) 234-4570

Paul's Boat Lines
(613) 225-6781

Bytown Pumper
(613) 736-9893

Watson's Mill
Mid-May to September:
Wednesday-Sunday 10:00-5:00
(613) 692-3571

Merrickville Blockhouse
Mid-June to September:
Daily 10:00-6:00
Closed Mondays
Spring and fall:
Saturday & Sunday 10:00-6:00
(613) 269-3614

Heritage House
May-January:
Daily 11:00-4:30
(613) 283-8560

Hershey's Chocolate
June-August:
Monday-Saturday 9:00-5:00
Sunday 10:00-4:00
September-May:
Monday-Friday 9:00-5:00
(613) 283-8800

33

SMITHS FALLS
By's Byway South

This second trip along Colonel By's canal takes us from from Smiths Falls to Kingston. Today's journey traverses a rugged, lake-dotted region verdant with pine and maple. This scenery combines with country inns and excellent museums for a pleasant outing any time of the year.

The day starts at the Rideau Canal Museum in Smiths Falls, overlooking the canal in the heart of town. Parks Canada has put its usual polish on this museum housed in a grist and saw-mill complex built during the mid-1800s. The main-floor lobby provides an overview of the canal with a huge model of the Ottawa-Kingston route, complete with lock stations, blockhouses and dams. Interactive video programs give plenty of pictures and details on construction, navigation and history for the 24 lock stations and 25 dams.

On an upper floor, visitors enter a tunnel where dioramas and videos describe the historic background of the canal. Overhear British generals plan a military supply route a safe distance from the American border; stand alongside By surveying a vast wilderness; watch the canal become a prime commercial shipping route; enjoy the age of luxury steamships when the Rideau was considered the best holiday in North America; grab the helm of a boat and steer it through the canal yourself (via video simulation).

You will leave the museum gung-ho to see By's accomplishment as it stands today. Take time to watch boats raised about 8 metres at the modern, electrically operated lock just outside. Signboards near the original three locks explain their design and operation. Across Beckwith Street from the locks is the Lockmaster's Boutique, a shop run by the Friends of the Rideau, a good place to pick up a souvenir drawing, map or book.

It's time to leave town, south along Highway 15 towards Kingston. (Railway buffs may want to see the Railway Museum on Abbott Street; ask for directions at the canal museum. Photographs, documents and several engines and railcars are on display. Visitors can board the Wickham car for a short journey.)

Travel south about 33 kilometres on Highway 15, making a left turn on County Road 9 to Chaffeys Locks. Head for the locks, a great spot to watch huge pleasure cruisers. Right next to the locks is the Lockmaster's Museum. These white frame houses with green trim occur at each lock station and were constructed to be defensible, with gun slits, fireproof tin roofs and thick stone walls at ground level. Museum displays focus on local history and the 24-hour-a-day job of the lockmaster.

Kingston Mills locks

The museum runs a video that is a delightful picture of this close-knit backwoods community that, from maple syrup to fishing, continues to live off the bounty of the lakes and forest. The show also features several Chaffeys' resorts which have hosted an international clientele for over a century. The tradition continues. Choose from the Opinicon Resort or Dorothy's Lodge, two fishing resorts still in family hands that are the pride of Chaffeys Locks. The Opinicon's varied menu includes prime rib, salmon steak and blueberry strudel. Dorothy's is touted by locals as having the best homestyle cooking around. Both resorts provide excellent service; reservations are suggested.

After trying your hand at the legendary bass of Rideau Lake, return to Highway 15 and drive south. Follow signs to Jones Falls, one of the prettiest lock stations along the canal. A lengthy pathway connects several historic sites. (The hills here are steep, so be prepared for a climb!)

The main draw at Jones Falls is the 19-metre-high, 107-metre-wide dam constructed to raise water levels to navigable depths. This was the first arched masonry dam in North America, the largest of its kind in the world. Technically impressive as well as beautiful, the dam is made of massive sandstone blocks, hand-cut to be very smooth and each joint perfectly fitted.

Visitors may tour the blacksmith's shop and lockmaster's house, both maintained and furnished as they appeared at the time of canal construction. The costumed guides are very familiar with their subject and the lockmaster's diary is a fascinating read. If you have left lunch until now, try Kenney's Hotel (1877) with Canadian specialties such as split-pea soup, rainbow trout and Nanaimo bars.

Drive south along Highway 15, exiting at County Road 21 to head towards Kingston Mills. This is the last lock site of the day and, as with the others, Parks Canada provides a pleasant picnic area, explanatory signboards

and a museum. This museum tells about life on the military frontier of Upper Canada through film, text and artifacts. Visit the small barracks, outfitted as a crude dining room on the first floor and soldier's dormitory on the second floor. Kids enjoy seeing the heavy, stiff wool uniforms, itchy blankets and simple pewter dishes used by the soldiers.

John By did not have daytrippers in mind while he toiled in the wilderness, but we will keep him in mind, grateful for the tremendous historic and natural resource he developed for Ontario.

Rideau Canal Museum
Mid-May to September:
Daily 10:00-7:00
September to mid-May:
Tuesday-Saturday 10:00-5:00
Sunday 10:00-5:00
(613) 284-0505

Smiths Falls Railway Museum
Mid-May to mid-October:
Daily 10:00-4:00
Otherwise by appointment
(613) 283-5696

The Opinicon
(613) 359-5233

Dorothy's Lodge
(613) 359-5811

Chaffeys Locks Museum
Late June to September:
Daily 9:00-5:30
(613) 359-5466

Jones Falls and Kingston Mills
Mid-May to September:
Daily 9:00-4:00
(613) 359-5377

34

FITZROY HARBOUR
A River Runs Through It

The Ottawa River is a principal artery in the heartland of Canada. Along its 1,250 kilometres of shoreline are all the elements that define the region: wilderness, lumber and mining towns, commuter suburbs and a sophisticated modern city. Begin a river-based day at the northern limit of the Region of Ottawa-Carleton and travel east along the river to the capital itself. Be sure to bring along a picnic lunch.

From Ottawa, drive west along Highway 17; exit at Regional Road 22, the Galetta Sideroad. A kilometre and a half past town is the signpost indicating a left turn to uncrowded Morris Island Conservation Area. (There are two good parks in the area for a picnic—choose between them.) Morris Island reflects many facets of the river's dramatic past. Iroquois Indians, fur traders and lumbermen all used the river as a transportation route, portaging inland at this point to avoid dangerous Chats Falls just east of the park. (The falls were silenced by a hydro dam in the 1920s.)

The conservation area provides several hiking trails through forest and wetland. The trails island-hop along the river via small bridges, and there are platforms for glorious views of the mighty Ottawa and the sheltered back bay. There's fishing for pike, pickerel and bass and canoeing in the bay. Some of the trails, washrooms and benches are accessible to wheelchairs.

The Mill Restaurant, Ottawa.

Return to Regional Road 22 and head east, following signs to Fitzroy Provincial Park. Fitzroy has a 2-kilometre hiking trail that meanders up and down steep terraces marking the river's glacial shoreline. The park is a good place for lunch; there is a mosquito-free picnic spot with a sweeping view of the river near the upper roadway.

Now it's time for some car-touring of the region. It sounds complicated, but just keep to the river and you can't go wrong. Continue along Road 22, turning south to follow Road 9 (also known as Dunrobin Road). There are small farms, forests, and posh commuter homes in the area, and occasional glimpses of the water. You will turn east, towards the river, along Road 129 and Road 21 (Torwood Drive). Finally, turn along Pinhey's Point Road.

Pinhey's Point is a ghost of a community on a very pretty stretch of the river. Hamnett Pinhey, a wealthy young blockade-runner, established an estate in the wilderness here in the 1820s. The remains include the 35-hectare grounds and home, many outbuildings and the evocative, ivy-covered ruins of St. Mary's Church (1827). (Guided tours of the church are available but no other public access to the ruin is allowed.)

The home has a ground-floor museum with changing displays on local history and the remarkable Pinhey family. One particularly interesting exhibit provides a vivid picture of a vanished era on the Ottawa River: the waterfront was busy with touring paddle-wheelers, mailboats and settlers in Durham boats. The grounds are accessible via guided tour or self-guiding brochure. The summer brings a wide range of special events, from art shows to live theatre.

Continue your downstream journey by travelling south to Riddell Drive, and when it joins March Road, follow it to Highway 417. The exit at 17B (Richmond Road to Carling Avenue) will link up to the Ottawa River Parkway, a quick and scenic way to the centre of the capital.

There are several places to admire the river rapids, the bane of explorer, logger, fur trader and settler. Voyageurs experienced in running the Ottawa River rapids were used by the British in Egypt to navigate the most dangerous stretches of the Nile River. Follow the river as the early adventurers did, to arrive at Victoria Island at the core of Ottawa. There are two places of interest to the traveller here. The first, located on the mainland just off the Parkway, is a restored grist mill, now the Mill Restaurant. Prime rib, steak, chicken and gigantic chocolate desserts are served at bargain prices. The 50-item Sunday brunch is very popular, as is lunch and dinner.

The stone ruins of several businesses are a second point of interest. From the mill, get onto the Portage Bridge; once on the Quebec side turn immediately left, and left again to gain access to Victoria Island. Many Ontarians do not know that Ottawa was once a major industrial centre, and the many old buildings here are interesting in themselves. But not to be missed is the detailed explanatory plaque describing several enterprises. Early Ontario capitalism began on Victoria Island with the Bronson sawmill (it produced over 70 million board-feet per year), the Ottawa Electric Street Railway (its powerhouse here also supplied the city with lighting), the E. B. Eddy plant and Willson's acetylene shop.

Take the opportunity to explore the Ottawa River shoreline. Not only will you visit reminders of history's major players—from glaciers to industrialists—but you will have a pleasant day to boot.

Morris Island Conservation Area
Open for walking year-round
Facilities operational
Mid-May to mid-October
(613) 259-2421

Fitzroy Provincial Park
(613) 623-5159 summer
(613) 836-1237 winter

Pinhey's Point
June-September:
Daily 9:00-5:00
(613) 832-4347

The Mill Restaurant
(613) 237-1311

35

OTTAWA
Downtown on the Farm

Life on the farm has altered radically over the decades, as family farms have evolved into agri-businesses. But one thing that hasn't changed is the pleasure of visiting a working farm. The Ottawa area has not one but two farms to enjoy. The Log Farm depicts life on a pioneer farmstead of the mid-1800s, while the Central Experimental Farm displays animals, crops and gardens developed through modern methods.

The Log Farm is located in the Stony Swamp Conservation Area. From Ottawa, take the Queensway to Richmond Road and exit south; drive to Baseline Road and make a left turn. Turn right at Cedarview and find Stony Swamp about 4 kilometres along. An interpretive centre is located beside the parking lot and the farm itself is reached by a pleasant woodland walk. (Take boots along during damp weather—the path is authentically muddy!)

Located on an original farm clearing, the Log Farm represents settler's life in the 1870s. James and Ann Bradley came to Stony Swamp mid-century and raised close to a dozen children in this home. Their life is described by costumed interpreters who guide visitors through the furnished house with its summer and winter kitchens, parlour and bedrooms. Children may participate in activities such as spinning, baking or churning butter. Outdoors, tasks such as the planting, harvesting and threshing of crops, vegetable gardening and tending of livestock are all carried on pioneer-style—and with more help from visitors. There are wagon rides and many special events, such as pioneer dances with live music. Log Farm staff make sure that all details, from the parlour wallpaper to varieties of field crops, are authentic to the period represented.

Then it's on to the Central Experimental Farm. Return to the Queensway, drive east and exit at Bronson southbound. At Carling turn right (west). Turn left at Maple Drive and follow the curving roadway to the parking lots near the Agricultural Museum. This is the best place to pick up farm maps and guides (a necessity) and find out the times of the horse-drawn wagon tours. The museum comprises several rooms devoted to the history of farm technology. Excellent explanatory text illuminates everyday farm topics such as hay baling for city-dwellers. The museum shop sells books on farming and gardening, T-shirts, posters and a host of small souvenir items.

Ottawa is unique among capital cities in having a working farm at its centre. In 1886 the national government recognized the need to advise new settlers on farming and livestock management. That was the first national experimental farm, which grew to include 500 hectares and 140 buildings and now attracts about half a million people from around the globe annually. Visitors will want to spend most of their time exploring the barns and gardens. Begin with the dairy barn. Adults are impressed with the immaculate condition of barns and livestock and children are thrilled to be in such close proximity to the animals. Next visit will be the beef cattle, swine and sheep barns. As in the dairy barn, all major Canadian breeds are represented and vital statistics such as size, weight, and milk or meat production are noted on display boards. The sheep barn is a highlight, especially during lambing season; it's hard to know which is more curious about the other, the visiting children or the lambs.

The Central Experimental Farm is not just animals. Down Maple Drive from the Agricultural Museum is a tropical greenhouse displaying more than 500 plants, from orchids to cacti. The building is resplendent with colour during the chrysanthemum show held annually each November.

For an overview of the farm take a Tally-ho Ride, a narrated tour on a Clydesdale-pulled wagon. The tour passes the experimental

Central Experimental Farm, Ottawa.

fields (where cereals and field crops are developed for greater disease resistance and hardiness), hedge gardens and ornamental gardens.

End an experimental farm visit by choosing whichever area interests you most, the arboretum or the ornamental gardens. The 35-hectare arboretum is home to over 2,000 varieties of trees and shrubs and is located on the hills surrounding Dow's Lake, across Prince of Wales Drive from the main part of the farm. The lookout points give a fine view of the lake, the Rideau Canal and Carleton University; walking trails traverse the arboretum.

The ornamental gardens are a must-see for serious home gardeners. Lively with bloom and perfume from May to October, the gardens are located on the west side of Prince of Wales Drive (just look for the wedding party posing for photographs). This is where new varieties of perennials and shrubs are tested, and many gardeners will recognize the

names of favourite roses, lilacs and forsythias developed to withstand our harsh winters. Of special interest are the two hedge gardens (named "old" and "new"). If you plan on starting a hedge, check out these areas for novel ideas.

Whether an old-fashioned pioneer farm or a sophisticated urban research centre, a day down on the farm was never so agreeable.

The Log Farm
Mid-May to October:
Saturday & Sunday 10:00-4:00
(613) 825-4352

Central Experimental Farm
Animal Barns and Greenhouses
Daily 9:00-4:00
(613) 995-9554

36

OTTAWA
A Capital City

One of the nation's premier tourist attractions is Parliament Hill. Day and night, winter and summer, throngs visit the "Hill" to gain a sense of nationhood, to express their opinion, to take part in civic celebrations. A visit to Parliament includes much, much more than the cliché snapshot with a Mountie, and a full day should be slotted for enjoying the Hill's many worthwhile sights and activities.

Parliament Hill refers to three buildings correctly but unimaginatively named Centre Block, East Block and West Block. The Centre Block is the well known building with the central clock tower that comprises the House of Commons and the Senate. Members of Parliament (MPs) have their offices in the East and West blocks, which flank the main structure.

Tours of the Centre Block are offered free of charge year-round, and are an excellent introduction to Parliament Hill. From the Victoria Day weekend until Labour Day, reservations are required and these are made at the striped Infotent just to the east of the Centre Block. (The incredibly well-organized Infotent should be the first stop for any summertime visitor arranging an itinerary.) During the remainder of the year, call the information office for details.

Personable tour guides present a capsule summary of Canadian civics and commentary on the architecture of the Parliament Building. The tour begins in the rotunda of the Centre Block, which is adorned with stone carvings of important national symbols and with official portraits of Prime Ministers. Visitors enter the House of Commons and get a close-up look at the familiar green-topped desks. If the House is in session, arrangements can be made to scrutinize the proceedings from the gallery. The staircase leading to the Prime Minister's office is part of the tour and is recognizable as the site of many a media "scrum."

For many, the highlight of the Centre Block tour is the circular library, the only portion of Parliament to survive the disastrous 1916 fire. The library is panelled with Ottawa Valley white pine; skilled carvers spent 20 years embellishing its beautiful surface. Documents and books are crammed three stories high, and the wrought-iron railings and provincial plaques lend a Victorian atmosphere.

Tours conclude in the Senate foyer where tour guides field questions from what is typically an interesting international collection of visitors. The foyer is decorated with royal portraits, the emblems of our founding cultures (England, Ireland, Scotland, Wales and France) and some unusual faces carved in stone (including those of the artists). Guides invite their guests to take the elevator to the top of the Peace Tower (the central clock tower) for a sweeping panorama of Parliament Hill and the Ottawa River.

If you time your sojourn to Parliament cleverly, you can leave Centre Block in time to view the 10 AM Changing of the Guard Ceremony on the manicured lawns in front of the building. This is a once-daily celebration of colour, music and tradition, as soldiers (summer students) perform drills and military march music. Many children rate this presentation—complete with blazing redcoats and bearskin busbies—as the climax of a capital trip. Guaranteed to stir the heart of first-timer and Ottawa resident alike.

The next call of the day should be the East Block—and no visitor to Ottawa should leave town before taking in this wonderful site. This "working" building has been altered little over the decades and, to the delight of historian and tourist alike, the offices of Sir John A. Macdonald, Sir George Etienne Cartier, the Governor General, and the Privy Council Chamber have been restored to their 1872 condition.

Parliament Hill

Macdonald's office is a delightful surprise in that the furnishings are not merely to period, but that the desk, chair, and lesser pieces are the very ones used by the Canadian legend himself. The tour describes an office life far removed from that of today—note the spittoon, the corner sink (cold water only, often frozen in winter), the coal fireplace and the pull rope to summon a secretary. Visitors often inquire about the oak doors connecting all the offices: in the age before central heating it was more pleasant to travel from one end of the building to the other by passing through all the private offices than through the bitterly cold corridors.

The Governor General's office is lavishly decorated with the trappings of Lord Dufferin, who held that office from 1872 to 1878. This chamber is more opulent than the Prime Minister's due to the Governor General's position as the Queen's representative, and this prestige is reflected in the turquoise and white cornices embellished with the Tudor

rose, stained glass windows, heavy curtains and a massive walnut partner's desk.

The wall panelling and other fittings in Cartier's office are similar to that in Macdonald's, an indication of their equal status as Fathers of Confederation. The room is arranged for a meeting, with the smaller chairs reserved for ladies positioned at the rear of the room, so that the wax-based makeup popular during the nineteenth century would not melt from the heat of the fireplace.

The last room on the East Block tour is the Privy Council Chamber, considered the most important historical room in the nation. These walls, with their ornate painting and gilding, have listened to 110 years of Canada's most controversial and agonizing debates and decisions, the cabinet meetings from 1866 to 1976. The voices of Macdonald, Laurier and Diefenbacher hang in the air. As in the former rooms, the decor is original, including the approximately

Front door, Supreme Court of Canada.

180-kilogram chandelier and the library of legal texts dating to the 1500s.

During the summer months, Infotent staff can book another tour for you. Titled "Discover the Hill," the outdoor walk takes in the exterior of Parliament, the Ottawa River and many splendid statues of historical figures. This is the best tour for appreciating how Gothic Parliament is perfectly suited to its dramatic cliff-top site. (This is a good point to note that public washrooms are located *underneath* the statue of Queen Victoria.)

The Château Laurier hotel just east of Parliament Hill has been eyewitness to so many important political and social events that is seems as integral to the Hill as Parliament itself. The architecture—steep copper roofs interrupted by dormers and towers—is a uniquely Canadian adaptation of the romantic French château. The

style proved so popular that it became synonymous with grand Canadian hotels across the country. The building is such a vital landmark, visually and historically, that tours are conducted through its public and private rooms on summer afternoons. The Château is named after Sir Wilfrid Laurier, Prime Minister at the time of construction, and his signature is first in the guest register (dated 1912).

There are two restaurants in the Château, and they are recommended for lunch today. Zoe's (named in memory of Sir Wilfrid's wife) is a casual tea room specializing in high tea. The dining room, Wilfrid's, offers an eclectic mix of international foods, from Chinese dumplings to gourmet burgers. The room recalls the days of Sir Wilfrid, with its tapestry carpets and chairs, etched glass windows and view of Parliament. While beautiful, the restaurant is decidedly family-friendly.

After a nutritious respite, visitors to Parliament Hill will want to continue exploring. Return to the Infotent to inquire about Capital Vignettes, outdoor theatre presentations focusing on key events and characters in Canadian history. Carillon concerts, played on the bells of the Peace Tower, are presented weekdays at lunchtime and on Tuesday and Thursday evenings during the summer. The Peace Tower instrument is considered one of the finest in the world, and the concerts are recommended.

For further insight into Canadian civics, walk west on Wellington Street to the Supreme Court. There are many glorious public buildings en route, such as the Langevin Block (corner of Metcalfe; this is the office of the Prime Minister), the Embassy of the United States, the National Press Building (which houses the Ottawa bureaus of most newspapers), the Confederation Building (note how perfectly it mimics Château Laurier) and St. Andrew's Presbyterian Church (1872).

The Supreme Court is positioned well away from the street scene, its art-deco severity chosen to express the neutrality of the court. Because the building's appearance is vastly different from the remainder of Wellington Street, the copper roof was added as an attempt to visually relate the edifice to the rest of governmental Ottawa.

Walk behind the building to take in the best view of the wide Ottawa River. To the west, near Victoria Island, is the location of Richmond Landing, the first settlement on this part of the river. Now return to the imposing front doors of the Court, and enter. Afternoon tours are offered during the summer while the court is in recess. During the remainder of the year, visitors are allowed to observe proceedings in any of the three courtrooms.

Half-hour Supreme Court tours are an information-packed overview of our highest court. Visitors hear details of how the court developed (it became our highest court of appeal at the late date of 1949), the selection of judges and our dual legal traditions of British common law and French civil law. Modern technology is revolutionizing the proceedings of the Supreme Court (for example, lawyers may present arguments via telecommunications hook-ups rather than in person), and this is also discussed. Displays in the foyer of the court describe the development of the law in each province.

Parliament Hill excursions need not retire with the sun, but can continue on well after dark with a "Sound and Light" show. Performances are presented in French and English on alternate evenings. Spectators sit on bleachers positioned immediately in front of the Centre Block and listen to a taped program of Canadian history, with actors taking the part of the Parliament Buildings themselves, various elements of our natural environment, and political figures. Lights of varying hues play on the Parliament Buildings and the Centre Block is completely enveloped in red during the portion of the show discussing the 1916 fire.

There's no doubt that the best place to appreciate our history and culture, in all its drama and debate, is on Parliament Hill. A day spent at the hub of the entire nation will evoke images to endure a lifetime. A capital day indeed.

Parliament Hill Information
(613) 992-4793

Centre Block tours
Daily, variable schedule

East Block tours
Mid-May to September:
Daily 9:00-5:00
September to mid-May:
Saturday & Sunday 9:00-5:00

Changing of the Guard
Mid-June to September:
Daily 10:00

Sound and Light Show
May-September:
Wednesday-Saturday varying hours

Supreme Court of Canada tours
May-August:
Daily 9:00-5:00
(613) 995-4330

37

OTTAWA
Food for a Capitalist

Byward Market is at the heart of Ottawa—both physically and socially—and it is no wonder that a city with a farmers' market at its centre is a city made for enjoying food. Join in a walking tour of Ottawa's market neighbourhood and celebrate the delights of food.

If you are not familiar with the market area, take along a street map. Navigate to the corner of Dalhousie and Murray to find Domus Housewares and Café. Domus is the place to find out about design trends in the kitchen and dining room without breaking your budget. An entire household could be outfitted from the range of dinnerware (first and second quality), trays, cookie jars, cotton rugs and so on. Microwave gear and an extensive selection of small appliances are also available. The cookbook section contains an exciting collection featuring cuisine from every corner of the globe. If the illustrations in the cookbooks have increased the appetite, then head to the small café adjoining the store, which concentrates on whole foods.

Ottawa's market has not only one, but two excellent housewares outlets. The second, Tinkers, is at 45 Clarence Street. Visit Tinker's for all the traditional and high-tech utensils you'll need for food preparation—the cook can no longer blame inadequate equipment. There are fondue sets and pasta pots, electric stirrers and ice crushers, copper-bottomed pans and punch bowls.

Number 103 Clarence is the address of Food for Thought, which began life as Ottawa's premier cookbook shop. Although the offerings have expanded into other topics, this remains a good place for chefs to browse, with books and magazines on cuisine, kitchen management and nutrition.

Snack time? Try Ottawa's own Beavertails from the booth at York and William. Don't be alarmed, these treats are not made from our industrious national symbol, but are large, deep-fried pancakes served with a variety of toppings; try the Killaloe Sunrise (lemon and sugar).

With shopping list in hand, head for the outdoor stalls of the market, which are tightly packed along Byward. (The arts and crafts stalls are inside the market building.) The market began in the 1840s as one of many sites where farmers congregated to display their wares. Ottawa's other markets have closed, but the Byward continues to increase in popularity. Producers from the Ottawa Valley and western Quebec sell a cornucopia of colourful, gleaming vegetables and fruit, maple syrup, honey and firewood daily. From the first tulips of spring through the gladiola of summer to autumn's Chinese lanterns and honesty, the Byward is enhanced by the offerings of several fresh flower vendors.

The best advice for a meal is to pick up the fixings for a picnic from the market stalls. As you peruse the outdoor stalls, make room in your basket for the specialty food shops along Byward. The following is but an appetizer: The Budapest Delicatessen stocks hams, cheese, crackers and crusty European breads, jams and mustards. Lapointe (fish merchants since 1867) adds a breath of the sea, with swordfish, tuna and salmon, smoked and fresh. The International Cheese House and the House of Cheese not only provide the picnicker with cheese (from Emmanthal to Cheshire) but also a variety of salads, olives, paté and breads. Freshly prepared fruit flans, tarts and other sweets are offered at Aux Délices.

Before embarking on a picnic, head for the cream of the market area, Stubbe Chocolates at 375 Dalhousie. The Stubbe family, European chocolate-makers for several centuries, brings to Ottawa an ample menu of heavenly treats, all made to high standards and sold at very modest prices. Choose from the likes of Williamtorte (chocolate sponge cake filled with cranberry jam and chocolate mousse, covered with milk chocolate) or Burgundytorte (Burgundy sponge cake filled with burgundy wine cream, covered with marzipan and red fondant).

Byward Market in the heart of Ottawa.

The market will provide a gourmet picnic hamper for your enjoyment, so it is a good thing that three novel parks are nearby. Within walking distance is Major's Hill Park (behind the Château Laurier), which dates to 1874 and was the location of Colonel By's house. The house is gone, but there remains a park with good views of the locks and Parliament Hill. Ottawa's daily noon gun is fired here (at 10 AM on Sundays). The end of the park closest to the Château is usually sheltered on a windy day and there are lots of benches for sitting.

Or there's Nepean Point (behind the National Gallery on Sussex). This park sits high above the Ottawa River, with great views of Hull, Parliament and the splendid gallery. There's an open-air theatre for summertime entertainment and a statue of Champlain and his famous astrolabe. If you prefer, you can drive to Rideau Falls. Drive north along Sussex past the Macdonald-Cartier Bridge; the park is on the river opposite Ottawa City Hall. The Rideau River enters the Ottawa River through twin waterfalls, aptly named from the French word for curtain. This is the greenest of the picnic sites recommended.

Spend a day at the Byward Market and discover a world of food fit for a king—or at least a Governor General.

38

OTTAWA
Science Trek

Ottawa is the place for techno-fiends, with two superb museums devoted to technology past, present and future: the National Museum of Science and Technology and the National Aviation Museum. To reach the Museum of Science and Technology, travel south from the Queensway (Highway 417) on St. Laurent Boulevard about 1.5 kilometres. Just look for the unusual lawn ornaments: a rocket, lighthouse and steam engine.

The Museum of Science and Technology should be the first visit of the day because, as any family can verify, a planned half-day tour often stretches into a full day. And at "Science and Tech," learning is packaged with a fun wrapping. Children run from one hands-on activity to another; exhibits flash and speak at passers-by like hawkers at a fair; announcements about various demonstrations come over the public address system.

A central museum theme is Canada in space. Canada was the third nation to enter the space age when the Alouette I satellite was launched in 1962. There has been no looking back, and Canadian expertise in adapting space technology for use in everyday life is underscored in exhibits on inventions such as remote sensing and solar cells. There are films on space robotics, toys in space, space food and lunar bases. Be sure to visit the display dealing with astronomy and its spectacular pictures of celestial scenery.

The history of communications technology is traced from early music boxes and gramophones

National Aviation Museum, Second World War section.

to fibre optics and lasers. Again, the emphasis is Canadian, with a history of CFRB (the first battery-free broadcast station in the world) and the use of satellites to end the isolation of small northern communities. There is a vast array of vacuum tubes, switchboards, antennas and the like. Canada's earliest radio broadcasts and television newsreel programs, which covered events from Red River floods to Pearl Harbour, are featured in detail.

The transportation area of the museum is another that combines activity and learning. Kids swarm through the gargantuan steam engines, and young and old alike are fascinated by the exhibits on navigation and shipping. They provide a look at Canada's illustrious maritime history; scores of historic boats, large and small; and navigational equipment. The excellent pictures and text concerning the luxurious but ill-fated *Titanic* are particularly captivating.

Three exhibit areas are perennial favourites: the Crazy Kitchen (the optical illusions are very realistic; visits recommended *before* eating), the incubator filled with hatching chicks, and the science gym where all the exhibits are kid-powered. Science in a more serious vein takes place during the evenings, when astronomy programs use Canada's largest refracting telescope.

Before heading out to the next stop in our techno-trip, make use of the museum's cafeteria (inside or outside seating, depending on the weather). Also be sure to take in Scientique, the wonderful store near the front entrance. Here there are clothes, books, toys, puzzles and posters, all with a scientific bent.

From Science and Tech, drive north on St. Laurent about as far as you can before turning right onto Hemlock Road, and continue from there to the Rockcliffe Air Base and the National Aviation Museum.

The newly refurbished museum houses one of the world's greatest collections of historic civilian and military aircraft. The first-rate displays, together with a busy schedule of films, demonstrations and hands-on activities, highlight the history of Canadian aviation. If you think that planes aren't exactly an exciting basis for a museum, this facility is sure to change your mind.

From immense tetrahedral kites to the Canadian planes mass-produced for the Royal Flying Corps in 1917, Canadian inventors and entrepreneurs were at the forefront during the early years of human flight. Our champions of the skies (from bush pilots to Air Force heroes) are profiled through historic photos, documents and film, and also through their flying machines. The collection includes the Silver Dart (reproduction), a DeHavilland Beaver, a JN-4 Canuck, and a Spitfire.

The size of Canada's immense territory meant that planes quickly became part of our culture. Exhibits detail the development of uniquely Canadian aircraft such as vehicles for landing on ice and water, air ambulances, bush planes and short take-off and landing jets. Our early entry into aviation meant that Canada became a world leader in aircraft design and manufacture.

There are exhibits on the recovery of historic aircraft, lighter-than-air machines (historic and contemporary), helicopters and air-traffic control. Each exhibit theme includes a video presentation (and/or computer game) that is initiated by the visitor, which means that there is no waiting for the next start time; longer films are held in a number of theatres around the museum. The Helicopter Studio is the perfect place for children to make paper airplanes, play with Lego and try out aviation puzzles, games and books. The museum shop, the Hobby House, carries a wide range of model kits for the enthusiast.

Our national contributions to the world of technology tell a story guaranteed to make even the most unassuming Canadian blush with patriotic pride. Enjoy the feeling at these two fine museums.

National Museum of Science
and Technology
May-August:
Daily 9:00-5:00
Thursday 9:00-9:00
September-April:
as above, closed Mondays
(613) 991-3044

National Aviation Museum
Hours as above
(613) 993-2010

39

OTTAWA
Homing in on History

Today's tour takes in three very different households, each one a showcase for its era. The Billings Estate, Laurier House and Rideau Hall are as distinctive, architecturally and historically, as three residences can be, making for an interesting home and garden tour.

The Billings Estate (circa 1828) was home to five generations of Billings, descendants of Braddish Billings and Lamira Dow, the first white settlers in Gloucester Township. "Park Hill" is a spacious Georgian home of white clapboard which still stands on its original site. The estate is on Cabot Avenue near Alta Vista and Riverside Drive; it's best to ask the locals for directions.

The ground floor of the house is a museum devoted to the lives and times of the Billings family. Expertly arranged displays of artifacts, diaries, photographs and games present a fascinating chronology of not only one family, but of an entire nation, as they follow the transformation of Bytown from unruly log town to a cosmopolitan centre of government. Tea and snacks are served under a marquee on the lawn, a good place for refreshments on today's trip. The Billing's Estate's eight acres of grounds (including flower gardens and the family cemetery) are a favourite spot for band concerts, Canada Day celebrations and Christmas carolling.

Our trip through time takes us to Laurier House, at the corner of Laurier Avenue East and Chapel. (Take Main Street to Colonel By Drive and from there to Laurier.) This yellow-brick Italianate-Second Empire house (1878) was witness to a large piece of Canadian history as the home of two prominent Prime Ministers, Sir Wilfrid Laurier (who lived here from 1897 to his death in 1919) and William Lyon Mackenzie King (resident from 1923 to his death in 1950).

Guided tours emphasize not only the house, but also the contribution of each Prime Minister to Canadian public life, as they struggled with national unity, economic expansion and international politics. Several second-floor rooms are dedicated to the Laurier years and feature original furnishings and stunning oak panelling.

Much of the house breathes of the era of Mackenzie King, and it is to his study that most visitors will be drawn. Here is the famous crystal ball, the portrait of the Prime Minister's mother (the portrait was the medium for communion between the two after her death), a guest book signed by dozens of notables, from Shirley Temple to Nehru, and an extensive library. King was quite a collector, and the house contains a unique assemblage of historic photographs (the rich, famous and powerful over four decades), paintings and furniture. The main-floor parlour and formal dining room are an opulently decorated glimpse into the social life of the Canadian elite. Laurier House also has a Lester B. Pearson wing which displays books, photographs, awards and other furnishings from our fourteenth Prime Minister.

The grandest home on the tour is Rideau Hall, residence of the Governor General. (Drive west on Laurier to King Edward and turn north. King Edward ends at Sussex/ Rockcliffe Parkway where you will head east and follow signs to Rideau Hall.) Guided walking tours of the grounds are available daily during the summer and on weekends spring and fall; tours of the interior are offered daily during the summer only.

The indoor tour begins in the marble terrazzo and stained-glass entryway with a brief introduction to the role of the Governor General and the history of Rideau Hall. Originally constructed as a family home in 1838, it was purchased by the government in 1868 for use by the head of state. It was our third Governor, Lord Dufferin, who added the tent room and ballroom in the 1870s.

The tent room is lined with the official portraits of most of the Governors General,

Mackenzie King's study, Laurier House.

and because the hall was originally used as an indoor tennis court, it is decorated with brightly striped circus-style fabric and gold tassels. Most Canadians will recognize the formal ballroom with its magnificent chandelier, made of 80,000 pieces of crystal, from television coverage of the Order of Canada ceremony. The tour includes the reception room, where much official business takes place, such as swearings-in and the presentation of ambassadors.

Outdoor features of interest include the fountain at the centre of the entrance drive and the Coat of Arms (the largest in the world) over the Hall's entrance. The highlight of the tour is the changing of the guard ceremony, which can be enjoyed at the entrance to the grounds and at the Hall itself. (Children scurry to follow the guards as they march from one end of the drive to the other, led by a kilted piper.)

The grounds of Rideau Hall are a lovely stroll. It is easy to imagine away a century, with a red-coated military band playing in the band shell, the guards marching up to the gatehouse and a cricket match on the field. What a splendid conclusion to a day of gracious homes and gardens.

Billings Estate Museum
May November:
Sunday-Thursday 12:00-5:00
(613) 564-1363

Laurier House
Tuesday-Saturday 9:00-5:00
Sunday 2:00-5:00
(613) 992-8142

Rideau Hall
Outdoor tours
Mid-June to August:
Daily 10:15-5:15
September-June:
Hours vary
House tours July & August:
Saturday & Sunday only, call for schedule
(613) 998-7113

40

OTTAWA
Art and Soul

Ottawa is a pilgrimage for patrons of the visual arts, with more public and private beauty per block than the world's famous art centres. The time invested in exploring the environs of Sussex Drive and the Byward Market brings rich dividends, since in this neighbourhood art takes centre stage—in galleries and studios, on buildings and street corners and even in a restaurant designed for art connoisseurs.

The National Gallery of Canada is housed in a splendid glass palace designed by Moshe Safdie, situated at the intersection of Sussex, Mackenzie and St. Patrick streets. While the size of the gallery and the collection—about 1,900 works are displayed at any time—is somewhat daunting, this is the best place in the country to survey paintings and sculpture from around the world and across the ages.

Be sure to pick up a floor plan at the entry desk and use it to locate galleries of interest. Canadian art is the focus on the first level of the building, with paintings from early Quebec to contemporary Canadian work. Don't miss visiting the remarkable Rideau Street Convent Chapel, with its vaulted ceiling and gilded screens. When this historic structure was delivered from the wrecker's ball and reassembled within the National Gallery, not only was a piece of architectural art preserved, but a deep sense of serenity was established at the very core of the facility.

The second floor presents an impressive spectacle of European art, from the Italian masters to Impressionism and Modernism. Whether you are an expert, or just someone who is learning to discern between a Titian and a Turner, this form of time travel is satisfying indeed.

Alas, one must leave the National Gallery sometime. For a distinct change of pace, visit the Canadian Museum of Caricature, situated kitty-corner from the National Gallery at 136 St. Patrick Street. (En route you may want to

The National Gallery of Canada.

admire the sculptures outside Notre Dame and perhaps look inside the cathedral at the excellent woodcarving.) Canadian political cartoons from the National Archives are arranged by theme and no cultural sacred cow, from peace-keeping to Johnny Canuck, is spared the satire of artists like Les Callan, Duncan Macpherson and Roy Peterson.

The Byward Market area provides a host of galleries; simply wander south along Sussex, taking in side streets from St. Patrick to George. Especially recommended is Murray Street, where Calligrammes, Hyperion, Darshan, and Gallery Lynda Greenburg all have changing displays of local and international paintings, sculpture, fabric and metal art.

This portion of Sussex Drive is referred to as the "mile of history"—and an evocative mile it is, too, with block after block of handsomely restored hotels and businesses dating to the mid-nineteenth century. Many of the structures conceal elegant stone courtyards, and most of these quiet spaces contain interesting sculpture. (Details on the wealth of public sculpture in Ottawa are found in *Sculpture Walks*, available at tourist information centres.)

For something completely different, visit the quiet square bounded by Sussex, Murray and Clarence. Once upon a time Ottawa tinsmith Foisy decorated his home with sheet metal made to imitate brick and stone; the facade is preserved in this quiet space, appropriately called Tin House Court.

The Ottawa School of Art, located at 55 George Street, often sponsors shows of student works. And one last site to visit is a tiny alley near Dalhousie and George where a wall mural, *Un Hommage aux Franco-Ontariens*, brightens an otherwise nondescript locale.

The best spot for an arty lunch is Santé Restaurant located on the second floor of the building at the corner of Sussex and Rideau streets. The walls are graced with the work of featured artists, and the tables are enlivened by culinary artistry called "fusion cooking" because it combines the cuisines of many cultures.

After lunch walk east on Rideau to Nicholas and then south two blocks to Daly. Arts Court is on the southeast corner. Formerly the Carleton County Court House (1872), this austere Italianate building is currently shared by various arts groups, such as film and television associations and performing troupes. The gallery portion houses changing exhibits by contemporary artists and the Firestone collection of over 1,500 works by the Group of Seven.

Onward to the last gallery of the day, the Canadian Museum of Contemporary Photography, tucked between the Château Laurier hotel and the Rideau Canal. Affiliated with both the National Film Board and the National Gallery, this museum boasts a collection of 157,000 works—photographs, books, mixed-media art—anything with a basis in still photography. The space and lighting have been specially designed with photographs in mind; the changing expositions vary in theme, from portraits of the Companions of the Order of Canada to women photographers.

Ottawa is a capital city that has room for more than just politics; its plentiful galleries provide much needed visual and spiritual refreshment. Take the opportunity to sample some fine art, Canadian style, in downtown Ottawa.

National Gallery
Daily 10:00-6:00
Thursday 10:00-8:00
(613) 990-1985

Museum of Caricature
Hours as above
(613) 992-9366

Arts Court
Tuesday-Friday 10:00-5:00
Thursday 10:00-8:00
Saturday & Sunday 12:00-5:00
(613) 233-3449

Santé
(613) 232-7113

Museum of Contemporary Photography
Mid-October to May:
Closed Monday and Tuesday
Wednesday and Thursday 11:00-8:00
Friday, Saturday & Sunday 11:00-5:00
May to Mid-October:
Friday-Tuesday 11:00-5:00
Wednesday 4:00-8:00
Thursday 11:00-8:00
(613) 990-8257

Sparks Street Mall.

OTTAWA
Around the World in a Single Day

There are wonderful benefits to life in a national capital. For one thing, an international subculture springs up as foreign embassies and their employees transplant a little piece of their own society to the capital. Add to this Canada's national character as a mixture of peoples from around the world, and Ottawa has developed an active and prominent international community.

Some of our cosmopolitan character can be experienced in Ottawa's "Chinatown" which, although small in population and extent, is a flourishing neighbourhood of people from across Asia. Drive or bike to Somerset Street West between Booth and Percy. The largest seller of Chinese foods is the Hong Kong Market at Arthur and Somerset. Loaded with items exotic (lily buds, lotus roots and essence of chicken) and commonplace (enormous bags of rice, noodles, oriental vegetables and fish), this market is an ideal place to put together an Oriental feast. Vendors along Somerset are customer friendly, so step right up and ask questions about food preparation and you will receive detailed answers.

Asian markets such as Yee's Oriental Gift provide hours of happy—and productive—rummaging for kites, chimes, silk and herbal medicines. Chinatown also provides a host of services to its community, such as acupuncturists, hairdressers, bookshops, barristers, and video stores.

There is a profusion of restaurants along this tiny strip of Somerset. Chinese restaurants offer fine meals in the style of Szechuan, Canton and Hong Kong. The two largest are Fuliwah and the Yangtze, which occupy opposite corners at Somerset and Cambridge. Each offers a varied menu including dim sum, which allows patrons to choose servings from trolleys brought to table-side. There are also Vietnamese restaurants, (well known for barbecued foods, noodles and robust coffees) and one restaurant from Korea, the Seoul House.

Chinatown is changing to reflect the influx of immigrants from other regions; there are businesses representing the Caribbean (Negril Tropical Foods), South Asia (India Food Centre, Nucreation Fashions and Lim Bangkok Grocery) and the Middle East (Middle East Bakery).

After an Oriental meal travel to Sparks Street, which runs east-west through downtown Ottawa one block south of Parliament Hill. Canada's first pedestrian mall, Sparks Street has two stores of special interest on today's trip. The House of Scotland (135 Sparks) is tailor-made for those pining for the Highlands. You'll find, of course, a multitude of tartan ties, kilts and other pieces of apparel, maps, tea towels and prints (historic and recent); less widely seen items include Island Rose perfume and Edinburgh Rock Candy.

Giraffe, a wonderfully intriguing store, is located at 67 Sparks. Crowded with traditional and modern arts from across the African continent, Giraffe is a most satisfying exploration. There are mud paintings from the Ivory Coast, batiks from Nigeria and amber jewellery from Ethiopia, and rugs, masks and baskets come from several countries. The wide price range means that there is plenty here for the casual buyer as well as the expert collector.

The final leg of our journey around the world within one city sends us to Rockcliffe Park, a prestigious Canadian address if ever there was one, and the location of choice for ambassadors. The Rockcliffe tour may be driven or biked. It is very pleasant biking terrain, and the biker has the advantage of being able to take shortcuts along Rockcliffe's many bike paths. In either case, a detailed road map will be a helpful companion.

Whether riding on two wheels or four, from downtown Ottawa travel east along Wellington to Sussex and head north. Sussex curves east as it enters what planners hope will become a sophisticated "embassy row." One of the first occupants, the modern Japanese Embassy, is at 255 Sussex, just down the street from the Lester B. Pearson Building, home to the Department of External Affairs.

Across the street from External Affairs and perched overlooking the Ottawa River is Earnscliffe, a Gothic Revival house with steep, decorated gables; it is the residence of the High Commissioner of the United Kingdom. Farther along Sussex, also on the river side, is the debonair granite-and-glass French Embassy. There should be no need to introduce Number 24 Sussex; the RCMP contingent posted at the entrance announces that this is the Prime Minister's residence. Immediately across from number 24 is the stone Embassy of South Africa.

Continue along Sussex and it becomes the Rockcliffe Parkway. The roadway and accompanying bike trails curve gracefully through wooded parkland and provide travellers with exceptional views of the Ottawa River. Stay in the centre lane of the Parkway until the *second* right turn, which is where the Parkway, Lisgar and Buena Vista meet; take Lisgar northbound (left). Don't worry about a wrong turn—all of Rockcliffe is worthy of a tour, so be willing to convert a missed direction into independent adventure. You many want to carry a copy of Kalman and Roaf's *Exploring Ottawa* with you for

interesting architectural and historical information on the houses along the route.

Number 420 Lisgar, a polished yet rustic wooden house, is the Danish Embassy. Continuing along Lisgar, the entrance to the residence of the U.S. ambassador is next on the right. If you go uphill along the road marked "no buses," the next estate of note is the lordly manor that is the home of the Apostolic Delegation to Canada. This château-style home was once occupied by Cairine Wilson, Canada's first woman senator. If the uphill detour was taken, return to Lisgar (which rejoins the Parkway after a bit) and then head right along Acacia. The embassies and ambassadorial residences will come at you thick and fast; the following is a small appetizer. (Note how many houses, whether built on a grand or modest scale, are Tudor in style.)

One of Rockcliffe's loveliest ambassadorial residences belongs to Japan, at 725 Acacia; the symbol of that country, the chrysanthemum, is figured over the stone archway. In the springtime, take the time to appreciate the daffodils in the "Rockeries" just across the street. The Indian High Commissioner's home is at 585 Acacia and the home for Korea is at 540. The residence of the leader of the opposition, Stornoway, is located at 541 Acacia. The ambassadorial residence for Thailand is at 439 Acacia and

Rockcliffe Park

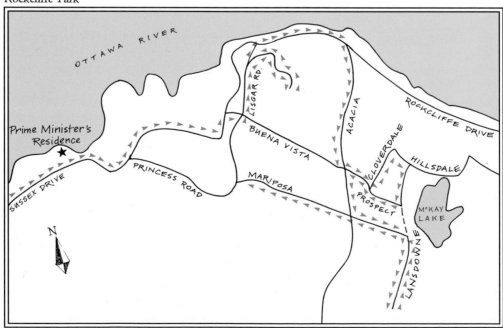

View of the French Embassy from Rideau Falls.

the residence for Benin at 488. Turn left onto Buena Vista and then left along Cloverdale.

Cloverdale curves east to become Hillsdale Road; turn right from Hillsdale onto Lansdowne. The Swiss embassy residence is at 494 Lansdowne, and the residence for Israel is further along at number 412. An Ottawa landmark, 400 Lansdowne, is Hart Massey House, designed by Massey himself in 1959. This unusual home, in the style of Mies van der Rohe, appears to float above the forested slopes that edge McKay Lake.

Cyclists may take the lakeside path to find the southern end of Lansdowne Road; drivers will have to follow the much less direct route along Prospect to Buena Vista to Mariposa and from there to Lansdowne South. Bulgaria's crest is found on number 190 and further along the street lies the Iraqi ambassador's home, identified by the imposing fence and gates. Number 120 is known as "Noot gedacht" (Dutch for "never thought") because when Princess Juliana of the Netherlands lived here in 1940 she never thought that she would be forced to flee her country. The house across the street at 115 was the retirement home of John Diefenbaker.

Return to Mariposa and head west (left). Renowned Ashbury College, located at 362 Mariposa, is a lovely Gothic-style school dating to 1912 and whose illustrious graduates include Governor General Roland Michener. (The counterpart for girls, the Elmwood School, is at 261 Buena Vista.) The Dutch flag flies over the house across the street at 361 Mariposa. Mariposa meets up with Lisgar, which was the starting point for this tour of Ottawa's finest neighbourhood.

Today's journey covered a wide variety of cultures, cuisines and residences—several dozen in only a few hours. Phineas Fogg could have made his trip less complicated if only he had put Ottawa on his itinerary.

OTTAWA
Natural Attractions

As befits a nation that prides itself on a squeaky-clean outdoors image, Ottawa has nature at both its centre and circumference. Nature buffs will adore a half day of discovery at the Museum of Nature in downtown Ottawa followed by a trek through the Mer Bleue Conservation Area in the eastern portion of Ottawa's green belt.

The Museum of Nature is located at Metcalfe and McLeod Streets. If you are travelling on the Queensway, exit at Metcalfe; from downtown, travel south on Elgin. Although it resembles an imposing turreted fortress, the museum is one of the city's most hospitable attractions. Each day, thousands visit to learn about the diverse natural history of Canada. High-quality exhibits (many visitor-activated)

and a lively public education program ensure that a large number of visitors return time and time again.

Mineralogy, palaeontology, botany, wildlife biology—natural science is here in all its diversity, and with a Canadian focus. The museum's collection is immense, and dates to the original Geological Survey initiated by Parliament in 1841 with the purpose of investigating and cataloguing the natural resources of the nation.

Dioramas depict flora and fauna in their natural setting, such as a wolf pack circling a bison herd or bats in a cave. For each habitat examined, text, photographs and diagrams are used to describe wildlife survival strategies,

Mer Bleue Conservation Area peat bog south of Ottawa.

predation, and the effects of pollution and human exploitation. One gallery has about a dozen full-size dinosaurs presented in their appropriate Western Canada setting. Those who live far from the ocean will appreciate the Bay of Fundy exhibit, which is a simulated tidal flat, complete with rhythmic surf and squishy sand footing.

Children will be eager to spend several hours at the Museum of Nature because so many activities are tailor-made for the see-touch-smell set. While to some minds mineralogy may be an adult-sized topic, the creative staff at this museum make it exciting for young children by having them travel down a mine elevator (complete with uneven momentum) on a quest for gold.

The two greatest kid-pleasers are the "Creepy Critters" gallery, where live insects and spiders from around the world are on display, and the "Discovery Den," where children pan for gold, dig for fossils and minerals in a sand pit, and work on science-related crafts. Kids delight in the year-round program of special events, from Easter-egg hunts to camping in the dinosaur pit. And that's not all—the museum is equipped with a science store (books, T-shirts, puzzles, kites, dinos, minerals, et cetera) and cafeteria.

After a morning appreciating the diversity of Canada's natural environment, take the afternoon to investigate firsthand a unique example of that diversity. Mer Bleue is a vast northern bog, a relic of the ice age, whose flora and fauna are typical of that found much farther north. Without a doubt, if you have time to visit only one of the capital's green areas, make it Mer Bleue.

Consider assembling a brown-bag lunch for an outdoors feast. Just north of the museum on Elgin is the Baker's Street Market, with custom-made sandwiches, salads and desserts, all for take-away. (There are plenty of restaurants on Elgin as well, from steak houses to bistros to Tex-Mex.)

To reach Mer Bleue, drive south on Metcalfe and take the Queensway (Highway 417) eastbound. Exit the expressway northbound at Anderson Road (Highway 27); drive along Ridge Road east to the Mer Bleue parking lot, picnic area and boardwalk. Before starting out on the trails, study the interpretive display near the parking lot in order to best enjoy the special beauty of Mer Bleue.

About 15,000 years ago, after the last ice age, this spot was covered by water; the sandy ridges separating the parking lot from the bog itself were islands in a wide river. Geologic and climatic factors led to the formation of a sphagnum and spruce bog covering thousands of hectares. Bogs cover only 12 per cent of Canada's land area and are characterized by, instead of a covering of soil, only a mat of slowly decomposing plant material that floats on water. Bog plants and animals have adapted to life in a highly acidic and nutrient-poor environment.

It is now time to enjoy the 1-kilometre boardwalk (closed in winter) that actually floats on top of the bog. No visitor leaves unimpressed by Mer Bleue, the uninterrupted expanse of low-growing sphagnum and leatherleaf (green in summer and rich cranberry-red in autumn), the quietude, and the opportunity to spot numerous birds, especially waterfowl. Those hankering to explore the Hudson's Bay Lowlands (the world's largest continuous bog) might visit Mer Bleue for an appetizer, since naturalists state that this area is very like that larger wilderness.

The numerous visitors who identify the Museum of Nature and the Mer Bleue Conservation Area as among Ottawa's greatest assets can't be wrong. Find out for yourself on your next day-outing in Ottawa, our natural—er, national—capital.

Museum of Nature
May-September:
Sunday, Monday and Thursday 9:30-8:00
Tuesday, Wednesday,
Friday & Saturday 9:30-5:00
September-April:
Daily 10:00-5:00
Thursday 10:00-8:00
(613) 996-3102

43

BROCKVILLE
Hostess with the Mostest

Brockville is a highly cordial daytrip destination. A riverside park, several historic sites and good restaurants have made Brockville a popular stop among Thousand Island visitors for many years. But best of all, a 35-room mansion, Fulford Place, has just opened to the public and is an impressive addition to Brockville's tourist line-up.

Begin the day at Brockville's busy harbour front. Armagh Sifton Park is a spacious waterfront development with a busy civic marina, playground, picnic sites and Canada's oldest railway tunnel. The tunnel, constructed between 1854 and 1860 and used until 1954, gave rail access to the harbour.

Take a pleasant stroll through the marina, a popular stopover for sailors and cruisers enjoying the St. Lawrence. Brockville is the enviable owner of 27 of the Thousand Islands, and they lie just offshore from the marina. Those with water transportation can pack a picnic and enjoy the lake breezes on the islands. Private transport can be arranged at several marinas and fishing resorts nearby; inquire at the tourist booth at the civic marina.

Walk uphill from the harbour to Water Street and head west several blocks to the Brockville Museum at Henry Street. This stone building dates to about 1840 and has several rooms of artifacts, photographs and text illustrating the town's history. Especially interesting displays deal with early industrial enterprises, such as the Stetson and Wolthausen Hat Company and the St. Lawrence Engine Company. The museum hosts special events each summer, including military displays, a strawberry social and children's workshops.

Just around the corner from the museum on Water Street is Shepherd's Mill Restaurant (1852), well known for its seafood crêpes, chocolate truffle cake and specialty coffees. From Water Street head north up John or Kincaid to the main street of town, King. Brockville is very proud of its historic

downtown and its fine nineteenth-century commercial buildings. There are plenty of interesting gift, clothing and antique stores. Apple Street just south of King is the location of the Towne Haus restaurant, a much-recommended (but pricey) restaurant specializing in continental cuisine.

Continue east along King Street to Broad and turn north to cobblestone Court House Square, a New England-style town square that faces onto a formal neoclassical courthouse, town green and a church on each corner. These buildings are even more impressive during the Symphony of Lights, when 25,000 bulbs flicker on historic buildings throughout the central core (held June to September and November to February).

Drive east on King Street several blocks. The lake shore was prime territory for the estates of the upper-crust. Brockville's pièce de résistance is a grey mansion called Fulford Place. Although much of the house is being renovated under the meticulous care of the Ontario Heritage Foundation, tours are available and are strongly recommended. When renovations have been completed, Fulford Place, furnished with 8,000 items, will be one of the most spectacular tourist sites in Ontario.

A visit to Fulford Place feels like stepping back the Edwardian era of gracious living and entertaining among Ontario's privileged class. Brockville is proud of its native son, George Fulford, who made a fortune in patent medicines ("Fulford's Little Pink Pills") during the late nineteenth and early twentieth century. Fulford didn't desert his roots, and built his home on a beautiful lakefront lot in Brockville.

Fulford Place exudes a distinctly masculine air, with dark and deeply carved panelling and ceilings and massive, simple furniture. Rooms are decorated in a variety of styles, from Tudor to French rococo and even flamboyant "mock-Moorish." Guides point out many interesting features, such as Oriental carpets, a

Brockville Festival of Lights

dragonfly-motif Tiffany lamp, and a clock (pre-1700) with porcelain numerals, a brass face and mother-of-pearl inlay. The brightest room of the house, the formal salon, is the only room where a lady's presence is primary, with Belgian silk tapestries, ivory carvings and Prussian enamel miniatures gathered on several global "grand tours." Most spectacular is the hand-painted silkwood Steinway piano.

The dining room is magnificent, the gleaming mahogany table meant to seat 48. Lavish entertaining was the rule of the day, and the Prince of Wales and all but two twentieth-century Canadian Prime Ministers have dined here. Apparently Mackenzie King attended his first séance at Fulford Place. Guides tell a good story about Mary Fulford calmly excusing herself from the dinner table, and Sir Wilfrid and Lady Laurier, to go upstairs and give birth to George Fulford II! When the Prince of Wales visited with the Fulford's, he usually stayed aboard the luxurious 138-foot yacht, *Magedoma*, a birthday gift from Mary to George Fulford.

Last but not least is the butler's pantry, which has an 2-metre vault that holds the exquisite silver service. The tableware collection includes a hand-painted set of porcelain especially manufactured as a gift for the Fulford's daughter. (A lovely estate just down the street was her wedding gift.) From sumptuous decor to a good history lesson, Fulford Place is a real treat for any traveller.

Like the Fulfords, Brockville knows how to be a gracious host, supplying a beautiful harbour, historic sites and good dining. Best of all, vistors to Brockville don't need a special invitation; just drop in anytime.

Brockville Museum
Mid-May to mid-October:
Monday-Saturday 9:00-5:00
Sunday 1:00-5:00
Mid-October to mid-May:
Monday-Friday 9:00-5:00
(613) 342-4397

Fulford Place
Saturday, Sunday, Wednesday 1:00-5:00
(613) 498-3003

44

PRESCOTT
Seaway Saga

The St. Lawrence Seaway, megaproject of the 1950s, was designed to provide central Canada with a reliable source of hydro-electricity and a link to global seaports. For the traveller of the 1990s, the Seaway furnishes a riverside drive that fills a day with pleasing scenery, unusual historic sites and plenty of outdoor activity.

Start a St. Lawrence day in Prescott, located at the western end of the Seaway. Prescott boasts three high-quality museums within easy walking distance of one another. The premier attraction, Fort Wellington, stands like a sentry overlooking the river, ever-watchful of the American shore a cannon's shot across the river. And a sentry it has been, since it was constructed to guard the critical St. Lawrence shipping route during the War of 1812. Pass through the gates into the fort and join garrison life in the 1840s.

The fort's largest structure is the blockhouse, with metre-thick stone walls and an upper balcony with trap doors to allow defenders to fire on anyone who managed to breach the ditch, earthworks and palisades. The blockhouse contains exhibits on the military history of Prescott. (One of these, a large model of the fort, is guaranteed to keep children occupied for a while.) During the War of 1812, the garrison captured the American town of Ogdensburg just across the river, and participated in the battle for Crysler's farm. The fortunes of the fort waxed and waned according to the state of relations between Britain and the United States, and the garrison was reactivated to take part in the Battle of the Windmill during the republican rebellions of the 1830s.

Tours of the fort include barracks, artillery storage rooms and the officer's building; the latter illustrates the relative comfort of the officers. The fort comes alive on summer weekends, with costumed presentations three times daily. A military pageant in mid-July (Canada's largest) brings to Fort Wellington noisy musket battles, a period military encampment and a wide range of hands-on activities.

When you leave Fort Wellington, walk west on Dibble Street one block to East Street. Turn south to find the Stockade Barracks and Hospital Museum. This Georgian home was built by Loyalist Edward Jessup in 1810 and was commandeered as a military barracks for British regulars and militia serving at Fort Wellington; it later served as a military hospital. It is Ontario's oldest barracks building still standing, and one of its oldest hospitals. A rarity among historic sites, the Stockade Barracks is a private, run-for-profit attraction that deserves a visit.

A tour of the Barracks Museum includes an excellent slide presentation on the War of 1812 and the role of the local garrison. The basement kitchen, complete with immense fireplace, is used during tours to describe barracks life and routine. Regimental life is reenacted in special barracks banquets and Georgian teas featuring period food and entertainment (by reservation only). The second storey has displays on the history of the hospital. Guides provide enough details concerning the hospital's use (many patients came here to recover from brutal corporeal punishment) and living conditions to make you queasy. (This modest homestead sheltered up to 100 men and almost as many horses and oxen.)

Now walk south on East Street and west on Water to find the Forwarders' Museum, a simple stucco-over-rubble building built in the 1820s. Prescott was favourably located at the western end of the notoriously vicious St. Lawrence rapids. Any lake ship arriving at Prescott (or ocean vessel arriving at Montreal) had to have its cargo reloaded onto flat-bottomed bateaux or Durham boats which were handled by tough and courageous boatmen to pass through the rapids. As settlers and goods from Europe went westward and colonial products such as salt

The Thousand Islands International Bridge across the St. Lawrence River.

pork, wheat, peas, lumber and potash travelled eastward, each trip padded the purses of forwarding companies, the entrepreneurs of the early nineteenth century.

Vital as the forwarders were to the development of Upper Canada, their warehouses, boats and crews were rendered obsolete by nineteenth-century canal builders. All that remains are St. Lawrence towns such as Prescott, and the forwarder's museum. Main-floor exhibits describe the travails of settlers and boatmen in overcoming the river. The exhibits also focus on the fortunes of the first forwarders, like William Gilkison, who used this very space as office and warehouse. The lower floor of the museum houses changing displays on life in early Upper Canada. You may want to ask museum staff for a walking-tour brochure of historic Prescott.

The remainder of the day will be spent moving eastward along the seaway. The river is smooth and sparkling where rapids once raged, and sailboats, fruit stands and river marshes fill the view once occupied by soldiers marching from Fort Wellington to engage rebels at the Battle of the Windmill. There are explanatory exhibits at the battle site, which is just off Highway 2.

Cardinal is a small village with a great view of the canal that was used to by-pass the river rapids. Cardinal also is home to the Coach House dining lounge, which is a lunchtime possibility if you decide not to picnic in one of the numerous riverside parks.

Continue your eastward drive to Iroquois. Upon entering town, head for the water and Iroquois' famous lock, the only Canadian deep-water lock on the St. Lawrence Seaway system. Signs provide details on lock size, lift and mechanics, and visitors are encouraged to watch small pleasure craft and huge

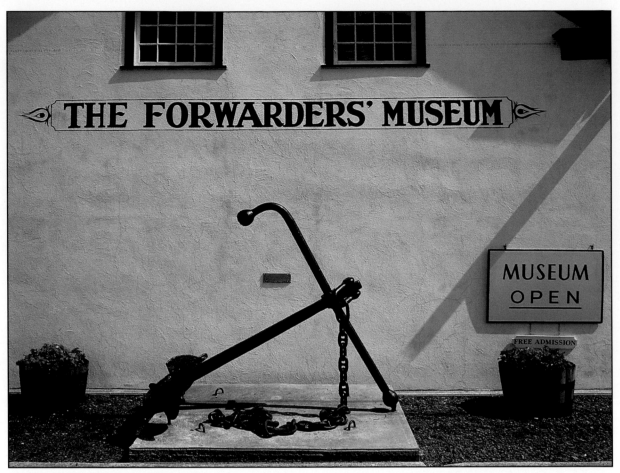

The Forwarders' Museum, Prescott.

international freighters pass. There are lock-side picnic tables and a snack bar.

Follow signs to the Carman House museum, a one-and-a-half-storey stone farmstead dating to about 1810. Carman House sits on its original site and features enough handsome carved mouldings, mantelpieces and original wallpaper to let us know that the Carmans were a family of some means. You'll be captivated by a video show about the building of the seaway and the consequent relocation of seven villages, the "lost villages" of the St. Lawrence. Almost all of Iroquois, situated between the Carman House and the river, was moved one mile north when Lake St. Lawrence was created as a head pond for the hydro station at Cornwall. Thus modern-day Carman House has a river view its builders did not enjoy.

Return to the highway and follow the St. Lawrence eastward. Just outside of Iroquois

turn south along County Road 4, which curves along the shoreline. You'll appreciate a close-hand look at some serene marshes (especially beautiful at dusk), and sometimes, the sight of children fishing and the scent of mown hay can add to the tranquility of the drive. Road 4 leads to Morrisburg, which has lots of restaurants and other tourist services to choose from, as well as a pretty waterfront park and a summer theatre. Near the water, on Gibson Lane, is the Old Authors' Farm bookshop which specializes in old, rare and used books.

Between Morrisburg and Ingleside there are plenty of attractions of interest. The St. Lawrence Parks Commission manages 1000 hectares of open space along the river and these lovely parks provide perfect picnicking sites and an abundance of recreation activities. There are public marinas, gardens, campgrounds and beaches, ski and snowmobile trails as well as the Upper Canada Golf Course (with dining facilities) and a nearby airstrip. As for events, there are organized nature programs, cross-country ski outings, and maple syrup and winter carnivals. The show-piece of the commission properties is Upper Canada Village, which rates a day of its own (see trip 46).

Once you have played yourself out, or relaxed near the shore, continue through the towns of Ingleside and Long Sault, created from the Seaway's "lost villages." The Long Sault Parkway connects these two villages and is a marvellously scenic drive or bike ride (see trip 47). Highway 2 leaves the river as it heads to Cornwall, the last and largest community on today's trip. Cornwall has a generous share of riverside parkland, and at its hub is a large marina, theatre and the Backstage Restaurant, where you can put your feet up and watch the river, with its cargo of yachts, freighters, speedboaters and anglers, go by.

A ramble along the St. Lawrence River is a unique opportunity to span Ontario's history—from musket-toting troops and rapid-running forwarders to the massive seaway construction project. History is so pleasant to encounter in such a beautiful locale. You'll be setting sail for the St. Lawrence again soon.

Fort Wellington
Mid-May to October:
Daily 10:00-5:00
(613) 925-2896

Stockade Barracks and Hospital Museum
June to October:
Saturday, Sunday
and holidays 10:00-5:00
(613) 925-4894

Forwarders' Museum
Mid-May to September:
Monday-Saturday 10:00-4:00
Sunday 12:00-4:00
(613) 925-5788

Carman House
June-September:
Daily 9:00-5:00
(613) 652-4808

45

KEMPTVILLE
Good Things Grow in Ontario

Southeastern Ontario is family farm country. The fertile, pastoral landscape has not succumbed to the urban sprawl and industrial agriculture so common in other parts of the province, making this a prime area for relaxing backroad drives and country walks. Kemptville is the epitome of a small agricultural service centre, and is a good base for farm-country touring.

Arrive in Kemptville via County Road 44 (it runs off Highway 16 between Kemptville and the 401). This turns into the town's main north-south street. At the south end of town is one of the region's most important institutions, the Kemptville Agricultural College. The 25-hectare campus is nicely landscaped and is a good place for a quiet walk during summer when classes are not in session. Visitors are free to visit the tropical greenhouse and livestock buildings. The most popular is the two-storey dairy barn; the 33-cow herd has been declared one of the best in the province. Children love to see the four-footed youngsters in the adjoining calf barn.

A tasty souvenir of farm country can be found at the farmers' market held Thursday evenings and Saturday mornings by the town hall in the centre of Kemptville.

Travel past the north end of town on Road 44. Kemptville's second claim to fame is the G. Howard Ferguson Forestry Station (named after the Ontario premier from Kemptville). Over 300 million trees have been grown here

Kemptville Agricultural College

since WWII, and these have been used to reforest private and public lands throughout Eastern Ontario.

The station's 527 hectares provide not only trees, but also lots of fresh air and five uncrowded trails. A brochure available at the forest-station office describes the trails, each of which offers something different. For example, the Turtle Trail passes a pond that is home to turtles and frogs, the Maple Trail is a good place for spotting white-tailed deer, and the Beech Trail is educational in purpose, and has identifying labels on the trees. Cycling is excellent on the station's many sandy roadways and the wintertime brings skiers, snowshoers and bird-watchers.

After a pleasant hike on needle-strewn paths, drive south on County Road 44 through town and turn west at Bedell Road. One-half kilometre along, stop at the agro-forest centre of Kemptville College. A brand-new facility, the centre is devoted to the role forest management plays in the farm landscape.

There is a 1-kilometre self-guiding trail with two dozen explanatory signs. These provide information on tree identification, the benefits to agriculture of forest management, and the influence of human activity on the forest. For example, as the trail traverses two 80-year-old pine plantations, one carefully groomed and the other left unmanaged, signs explain the benefits of tree pruning. Reforested fields are used to illustrate the role of windbreaks and hedgerows in soil conservation. The maple bush is very active during the spring and the interpretive centre building includes a full syrup operation.

Leave the agro-forest centre and drive west along Bedell Road. A short drive away is Evergreen Farm, a real find for people who love growing things. The owners, Larry and Anstace Esmonde-White, are well known to devotees of gardening shows: they host *From a Country Garden* on PBS and are frequent guests on CBC *Midday*. The television programs are filmed at this property. The gardens are open to the public on the weekends at a very modest charge.

Evergreen Farm is saturated with loveliness. The gardens are not large, but have been designed as many secluded outdoor "rooms";

this maximizes the number of different viewing points. You can enjoy gardens especially designed for season (the spring garden), colour (the blue and white garden, rich with clematis, iris and peony), scent (thyme square) and food production (the show-piece vegetable garden, orchard and herb gardens). Children will not want to (or may not be able to) leave the excellent and aromatic cedar maze. Just when you think you have seen the best garden of all (perhaps the marvellous roses) another special place appears around a corner, perhaps the water or shrub garden.

Evergreen Farm is first and foremost a working garden. This is the place to learn how to construct compost bins, prune for good fruit production, choose tools appropriate for your needs or use cold frames. The ultimate nirvana for the green-thumb set.

There comes a time when you must reluctantly leave Evergreen Farm. The only reward is knowing that a good meal is just ahead. Continue west on Bedell Road to the somnolent village of Oxford Mills. The Brigadoon Restaurant is located right "downtown." This handsome stone building made bright with geraniums was constructed as a general store and post office in 1842. The Sunday brunch is very popular with daytrippers, who travel here by auto or bicycle. The Brigadoon also serves afternoon tea, lunch buffets and prime-rib dinner buffets. The menu features pot pie, steak, seafood and pasta; leave room for amaretto ravioli or Brigadoon ice-cream pie.

From pine trees to Holsteins, primula to strawberries, Kemptville and area prove that good things do grow in Ontario!

Kemptville College of Agriculture
Grounds open daily
(613) 258-8431

G. Howard Forest Station
Grounds open daily
(613) 258-8355

Brigadoon Restaurant
(613) 258-4433

46

MORRISBURG
The Good Old Days

The queen of Ontario's pioneer villages is Upper Canada Village near Morrisburg. This status comes from not only the sheer number of buildings—over 30—but because, from the ring of a blacksmith's hammer to the creaking millwheel, this is a living community and not a static display. Plan on spending an entire day at the village. (Those in an unseemly twentieth-century rush may consult the visitor guide for ideas on abbreviated tours.)

Twenty-seven hectares of buildings, waterways, roads and farms represent a St. Lawrence community of about 500 people during the 1860s. Each building is an original, most having been rescued from the rising waters of the river following the construction of the seaway and dam at Cornwall. Bordered by the river along one side and a large rose garden on another, the village is buffered from any sign of modern life.

The focus of village life is agriculture and the two working farms, one a modest tenant farm and the other, the Loucks' farm, a more prosperous enterprise. The farms can be contrasted by the comparative luxury (or lack thereof!) of the houses, quality of livestock and cultivation methods (manual versus horse-powered machinery). The Loucks' farm is complete with large barn, drive shed, poultry shed, smokehouse and hired hands' home. Children appreciate the opportunity to wander through the sheds, and discover piglets and chicks, and operate the hand pump. At the Upper Canada cheese factory, tourists can get an up-close look at manual cheese-making, which is performed every day but Sunday.

Near the farms is the education centre, a sure hit with kids, who may try their hand at pioneer crafts and games, model children's clothing from the past century and use a quill pen. This is also the spot to catch the horse-drawn bateau that travels a canal from the tea garden to the riverside signal tower.

The main streets of the village are lined with several enterprises: a printing office, physician, cabinetmaker, bakery, shoemaker, blacksmith, tinsmith, tavern and general store. Other attractions include two churches (Christ Church and Providence Chapel) and a school.

In each building costumed guides do more than provide a tour, each guide lives their part. Don't miss the performance of the schoolmarm, who makes her "students" squirm with her stern reprimands. The printer describes the laborious job of typesetting by hand (the paper produced here is central to the interpretive program, be sure to pick one up). In the Lutheran pastor's home, the pastor, complete with German accent, arrives to discuss parish work with visitors. And in Cook's Tavern, women are made fully aware of their lesser status, when they are led to a small plain waiting room quite separate from the main pub.

When it approaches time for a midday meal, there are two choices. The Harvest Barn is located near the printing office and is cafeteria style. Better yet is Williard's Hotel, which offers table service and items such as chicken pot pie, roast duckling, ploughman's lunch and johnny cake with maple syrup. Patrons relax and observe the horse-drawn lawn mower trimming the fairgrounds across the street, or listen to the rattle of the yellow stage-coach as it makes its way down Queen Street. (Reservations advised during summer weekends.)

Manufacturing activity in the village is concentrated in three mills, and they earn their living honestly. Village bread is baked with flour ground in the grist mill, and shingles and other lumber required around the village are sawn daily in the lumber mill, and the blankets sold in the gift shop are made from wool processed in the woollen mill.

Although you may have toured many mills before, this is your best chance to get very close to a saw as it makes its slow progress

Upper Canada Village

through an enormous tree or to hear the work whistle signalling break-time for the women and children labouring over looms at the woollen mill. Each mill is a fascinating exploration of machinery, water power and steam power (the flour mill is run by steam) Upper Canada Village millers are experts in their trade, and visitors from far and wide seek their advice on matters such as lumber to be used in restoration projects. The serene mill pond completes the setting—weeping willows, ducks, goldfish and all.

If all this is not enough to stimulate tourists, Upper Canada Village runs a full schedule of special events from Victoria Day to fall fairs. A new attraction is the Upper Canada Railroad, a replica wood-burning train that transports passengers on a slow-motion 2-kilometre trip from the village to Crysler Beach and Marina. Before exiting the village, visit the gift shop with its supply of village-produced baked goods, cheese and woollens as well as an extensive stock of books on all things historical.

While every guest at Upper Canada Village might choose a different building or activity as their favourite, all agree that it is the meticulous attention to detail that makes the settlement such a worthwhile visit. The child with shawl and basket heading for the bakery, the aroma of freshly made candles and currant jam; the white picket fences and snaky split rails—all these make the village the best recreation of nineteenth-century Ontario anywhere.

Upper Canada Village
Mid-May to mid-October:
Daily 9:30-5:00
(613) 543-3704

47

LONG SAULT
Spinning Wheels

With kilometres of unexplored territory ahead and a breeze on your face, there are few things as exhilarating as cycling. South-eastern Ontario is beloved by cyclists, who appreciate its level terrain, low-traffic backroads and frequently encountered points of interest.

We are indebted to clever planners who laid out a paved bike path approximately 20 kilometres in length from Cornwall's waterfront west to the Long Sault Parkway. Not only is it good cycling, but it reveals the story of the "lost villages of the St. Lawrence"—communities erased forever by the rising waters of the St. Lawrence after the construction of a hydro dam and seaway.

The route is described from east to west, beginning at the R. H. Saunders Power Dam on Cornwall's western perimeter. There are great views of the river here and some of the large industrial complexes tht have been attracted to the region as a result of the power project.

Hop on your bicycle and head west on the signposted bike path for some pleasant, flat-land cycling. There are plenty of parks en route with picnic spots and washrooms. The trail winds along Highway 2, sometimes through lightly wooded areas, and sometimes through open meadow scented by wildflowers. Roadside fruit and veg stands offer tasty mementos of the day, from spring strawberries to the last pumpkin of fall.

Ault Park is near Long Sault, and is the site of the log-cabin home of the Lost Villages

Long Sault Parkway across the St. Lawrence River.

Historical Society. Changing exhibits—mock-ups of stores, churches, schools, railway stations—illustrate life in the villages flooded by the seaway project. The museum has scores of neatly organized photograph albums that are well worth perusing. There are pictures of intrepid canoeists challenging the infamous Long Sault rapids, of huge Victorian homes hoisted onto truck for removal (or being burned if they could not be moved) and of "Inundation Day" when tourists flocked to watch while the retaining dam was dynamited and water slowly seeped over the landscape.

The albums bear mute testimony to the quiet charm of the villages before resettlement. Moulinette and Mille Roches became the new town of Long Sault, while Dickenson's Landing, Wales, Farran's Point and Aultsville became Ingleside. Iroquois and Morrisburg were partially relocated, but their story is best found at Carman House in Iroquois. You may be intrigued enough to read *Bowering's Guide to Eastern Ontario*, with its excellent chapter on the lost villages.

Continue along to the beginning of the Long Sault Parkway, which connects Long Sault and Ingleside. (At the entrance is the Country Bakery, a good place to pick up homemade soup, sandwiches and delectable sweets.) The parkway is wonderful cycling: it hops from island to island, each tiny isle the remainder of a pre-flood hilltop. There is always a fresh breeze off the river, as you pass by numerous still lagoons with poised herons and some of Ontario's prettiest picnic spots. The white sand beaches are welcome on a hot day, but they can be very congested on weekends.

It is on the Long Sault Parkway that you can see the location of several of the lost villages. One of the first islands is Macdonell Island. Cycle to the southernmost tip of the island, where there is an excellent display of text, photographs and maps telling the story of seaway construction. The river narrows just south of the island and the water churned through here as the notorious Long Sault rapids, which were silenced by the deepening of the river. There is a yellow rope marking the beginning of a dive trail linking underwater remains of the villages, such as lock stations and dams. Wet-suited divers can be seen entering the water to explore Lock 21 of the old Cornwall canal located just off shore.

As you ride west along the parkway, you will notice paved and gravel remnants of the original Highway 2 leading off into the water. And in the waters between the parkway and the mainland is a dive buoy marking the location of Dickenson's Landing. At the western terminus of the Long Sault Parkway, either return to Cornwall or keep on cycling to two more sites.

West along Highway 2 is Farran Park. Drive to the parking lot furthest south. The line of tall pines along the parking lot's edge marks a house lot that was part of the town of Farran's Point. Locals say that when the water is low, you can walk along the sidewalks and driveways of the village, located just southwest of the park.

Cycle westward to the Upper Canada Bird Sanctuary. The paved entrance road was the original roadway heading down to riverside Aultsville, the prettiest of the lost villages. When the road veers left, ride straight ahead to the edge of an old railroad route. Look carefully, and you will see the sidewalks of Aultsville half-hidden among the pavement and shrubs. Before leaving the sanctuary, you will want to visit the lookout tower for a view of the vast marshes which support a diverse population of ducks, geese and other waterfowl. Sanctuary staff run a busy schedule of special events year-round.

You've not only had a wonderful day of fresh air and exercise, but you've done it without polluting the environment and by appreciating one of eastern Ontario's greatest stories—the lost villages of the St. Lawrence.

Lost Villages Historical Society Museum
July & August:
Wednesday-Sunday 10:00-5:00
(613) 534-2197

48

MAXVILLE
A Highland Fling

In 1786 parish priest Alexander MacDonell led a party of 500 Scots Highlanders to the green hills along the Raisin River. Together with later arrivals, who often emigrated as entire clans led by a chieftain, they established Glengarry County as a stronghold of Gaelic culture. That culture is as vibrant today as it was two centuries ago and makes Glengarry a good destination for anyone seeking the Scottish side of Ontario's character.

Begin in tiny Dunvegan, located at the intersection of County Roads 30 and 24 just south of Highway 417. The Glengarry Pioneer Museum's main building was originally a log store which became the Star Inn around 1840; the barroom is still intact. The collection focuses on furniture, implements and clothing used by area settlers. The library has an interesting selection of Gaelic Bibles and books written by the area's many authors. The museum houses a wealth of settlement records, notes of council meetings, church records and early maps for those doing genealogical research.

Drive west on Road 24 to Road 20 and turn south towards Maxville. Local legend has it that the town is so-named because almost all the inhabitants had surnames beginning with Mac. Early census takers would have agreed: the most common names in the last century were MacDonald, McDonell, MacMillan, MacDougall and MacLeod. Any country sideroad drive will reveal how intensely Scottish the area has remained, so many mailboxes bear these exact names, and farmers work the same land cleared by their ancestors.

Maxville is famous for its mammoth Highland Games (held annually in August) which draw an appreciative international audience. You will be thrilled by the sound of massed pipe-and-drum bands and sway in time to the Highland dances. The track-and-field competition includes events unfamiliar to many, such as caber and sheaf tosses, and stone and hammer throws.

Danskin's Scottish Gift Shop, located on Main Street, is an excellent source for those searching for a particular tartan, whether as a piece or to be custom-made into a vest, kilt, jacket or cap. Highland dance shoes, piping supplies, clan jewellery, Scottish music, books and china are also available.

Follow County Road 20 south to Highway 43 and turn east. Continue on to Alexandria, named after aforementioned Alexander MacDonell, who became the first Bishop of Upper Canada. Alexandria's Georgian House 1858 Restaurant is recommended for friendly service, an historic setting and edibles such as lobster or salmon in pastry, steak tartar, or house speciality pork bohemian (cooked with garlic and mushrooms).

Proceed on your Highland fling by driving south from Alexandria on Highway 34. Directional signs indicate a westward turn on County Road 18 to St. Raphael's Ruins (1815). This enormous grey stone church, built without interior pillars or nails, served for a time as the centre of Roman Catholicism in Upper Canada. A 1970 fire gutted the interior, but the walls remain and the ruin can be freely explored. Perched on a small knoll above fragrant meadows and companioned by a large graveyard, lofty St. Raphael's leaves a distinctly romantic impression.

After a stroll at St. Raphael's, drive west on County Road 18 to County Road 19 and from there south to Williamstown, located on the Raisin River. Old by Ontario standards, Williamstown began as a mill village in the 1790s. Williamstown's Presbyterian Church was the first built in Upper Canada (1812) and Ontario's oldest fall fair is held here, annually since 1808.

Williamstown was the heart and soul of Canada's fur-trading industry. A number of the famous North West Company's leaders retired here, and countless explorers and traders were drawn from the local Scots community. The Nor'Westers and Loyalist

Maxville's famous Highland Games.

Museum is located on John Street. The museum highlights the ruthless and restless nature of these men who explored Canada's wilderness, conquered half a continent and built a vast commercial enterprise. The museum chronicles the careers of Nor'Westers such as David Thompson and Simon Fraser. Personal effects and equipment, journals and pictures afford the visitor a window into the trials and triumphs of Canada's early explorers. The museum also has exhibits on the politics, social life, education and economy of Glengarry's Loyalist pioneers.

Williamstown has another site of interest—Thompson-Bethune House, home of David Thompson, and earlier, Reverend John Bethune, Upper Canada's first Presbyterian minister. Ontario's oldest domestic structure, Thompson-Bethune House dates to 1784, the period of the first Loyalist settlement. It is a Georgian cottage (although the porch added by Thompson is Regency) and the interior is virtually unchanged since 1804. This house has been home to many generations of prominent Canadians, and is worth a visit to hear of their histories.

After a day spent touring Glengarry County, you'll agree with the observation of local writer Dorothy Dumbrille: "The day old

Scotland's heart was torn, A little piece of it was thrown Across the sea to Canada, Who reached a' clasped to her own."

Glengarry Pioneer Museum
Mid-May to July and
September to mid-October:
Saturday & Sunday 1:00-6:00
July & August:
Tuesday-Sunday 1:00-6:00
(613) 527-5230

Maxville Highland Games
(613) 527-2876

Georgian House 1858
Closed Mondays
(613) 525-2219

Nor'Westers and Loyalist Museum
Mid-May to September:
Monday-Friday 1:00-5:30
Saturday & Sunday 10:00-5:30
September to mid-October:
Saturday & Sunday 1:00-5:30
(613) 347-3547

Thompson-Bethune House
Sundays 1:30-5:00
(613) 347-7192

49

CORNWALL
Warp and Weave

Cornwall capitalizes on its status as the manufacturing hub of Eastern Ontario to provide tourists with a day of industrial history, museums and a distinctly different factory tour.

Local history is the focus at the United Counties Museum, located on Second Avenue West. If travelling via the 401, exit south at Brookdale Avenue and turn west at Second Avenue. The museum is in the home of Loyalist William Wood, who settled this land in the early 1800s; his descendants lived here until the mid-1900s. How surprised the first Woods would be to find their rural farmhouse dwarfed by gargantuan factories and hemmed in by railway tracks. It may be an appropriate location, however, for a museum devoted to Cornwall, since the story of this city reflects the course of industrialization over the past 150 years.

Wood House has two floors of furniture, clothing, household implements and toys depicting life in nineteenth-century Ontario. There is an engrossing display on textile manufacturing, which began in Cornwall during the 1860s, when prosperous investors were attracted by cheap water power and the Cornwall canal. There are vivid descriptions of the tortuous working and living conditions endured by mill labourers and the attempts by church and state to provide housing and social services. Lastly, there are exhibits on the history of electrification in Cornwall. The Canada Cotton Mill was the first plant in the world lit by electricity and the installation was supervised by Thomas Edison himself.

Once set on the path towards being a manufacturing city, Cornwall continued to attract a diversity of companies. One present-

Cornwall

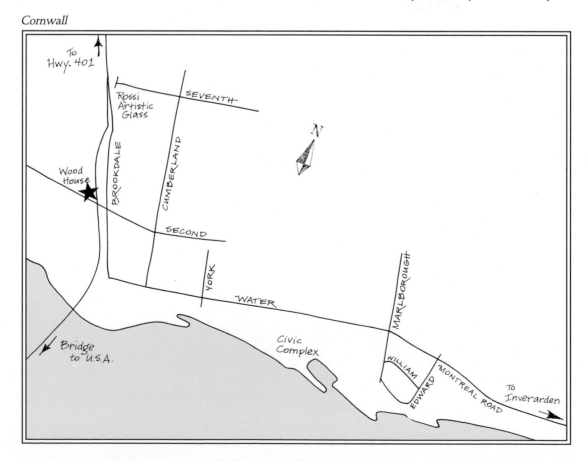

day firm plays host to locals and tourists alike, providing an up-close look at the art and science of glass-blowing. From the Wood House, drive east to Cumberland Street and then north to Seventh Street; turn west to find number 450, Rossi Artistic Glass. Congenial guides give a brief tour of the shop floor, with its blazing furnaces and shelves of cooling products. Visitors watch as a demonstrator makes a few brisk movements and a plug of glowing, molten glass is blown and snipped into a horse, a flower, or a bird. The pieces created during the tour are handed out as souvenirs. Guests are invited to try their hand at glass-blowing and to peruse the showroom.

The following driving tour will take you through Cornwall's historic industrial area. From Rossi Glass, drive south on Cumberland and east on Water Street. (At the corner of York and Water, note the row housing constructed to house mill-workers during the 1880s.) Cornwall has several kilometres of waterfront parks which culminate in the civic complex (arena, theatre and marina); the centre's restaurant, the Backstage, has a river view, summertime volleyball court and good pub grub. Continue along Water Street (its name changes to Montreal Road) which will take you to the heart of mill town, east-end Cornwall. Thousands of French-Canadian textile workers resided here; to this day the neighbourhood retains a strongly Francophone atmosphere.

Turn south on Marlborough Street and then east along William Street. On the right is the Dundas Mill (Cornwall Manufacturing Company), topped by a bell tower. The mill was built in 1870 and its large scale and architecture are typical of east-end Cornwall plants of the last century. On the left is the Deruchie Foundry, established to provide parts for the booming textile manufacturers; the plant has been significantly altered.

As you head north on Edward Street, pause to appreciate the beautiful, Italianate-style Canada Cotton plant (1872). The weave shed was the largest built in Canada and is the factory where Edison oversaw electric-light installation. As did the other textile mills, Canada Cotton closed about 25 years ago. Continue east along Montreal Road. At Danis Road is the Courtaulds plant, Canada's first rayon factory, opened in 1924.

The next stop of the day is historic Inverarden, a home turned museum. Drive east past the outskirts of town, where Montreal Road becomes Highway 2. Inverarden is located near Boundary Road. This home of Nor'Wester John McDonald was constructed in 1816 in a Regency style meant to mimic the "cottages" of Imperial India. Inverarden is considered the finest example of this form in Ontario. It is characterized by a single storey with a hip roof; tall, paired windows; and balanced chimneys (chimneys symmetrically placed on each side of the house).

Nine rooms are furnished in the style of the 1820s period. This retirement estate is filled with some of the loveliest antiques you can see in Eastern Ontario: portraits and maps dealing with the North West Company, finely turned mahogany chairs and a dining room gleaming with silver, from tableware to candelabra. Each room contains detailed notes on the furnishings.

Inverarden Regency Cottage Museum staff provide visitors with slide shows on local history and architecture. A program of special events runs from April to November and features cooking, crafts, sports and music from the nineteenth century.

For one last taste of the Cornwall region, drive ten minutes east from Inverarden to the hamlet of Glen Water and the Glendale Tavern. This is a well-known spot for a local specialty, perch rolls, made with fresh St. Lawrence perch. Well worth a visit to soak up some local flavour.

United Counties Museum (Wood House)
April to mid-November:
Tuesday-Saturday 11:00-5:00
Sunday 1:00-5:00
(613) 932-2381

Rossi Artistic Glass
Weekends only by appointment
(613) 938-7760

Inverarden Regency Cottage Museum
April-November:
Monday-Saturday 11:00-5:00
(613) 938-9585

L'ORIGNAL
Only the Château Knows

Ontario's easternmost region is an interesting area to explore. While there is an unmistakable French influence, this is a truly bicultural place where residents move between French and English with enviable ease. Today's journey ventures along the lower Ottawa River, from the capital to the Quebec border.

Exit Ottawa by way of Highway 17 eastbound. As the road nears Cumberland it curves to follow the water, and it is here that we join the original river road constructed a century-and-a-half ago to connect villages served only by steamship. Slow down and enjoy, for the view is fine in any weather, whether the river islands are shrouded in mist or brilliant with fall colour.

Cumberland is one of two original river colonies seen today (the other is Lefaivre) and several fine houses on the original main street signify its early prominence. The Cumberland Township Heritage Museum is the first stop of the day. From Highway 17, turn south (*away* from the river) to the main intersection of town; turn left (east) and follow signs to the musuem. The 40-hectare site includes over 15 buildings, such as houses, businesses, a church, a school and a railway station. Special events, costumed staff and exhibits illustrate the township's history from 1880 to 1935.

Continue along Highway 17 to Rockland, where you will leave the highway and follow signs to tiny Clarence. Continue alongside the river until Jessups Falls, where you will rejoin Highway 17 momentarily and then leave it again to head north to the river. Throughout this area, the landscape is more characteristic of seigneurial Quebec than Ontario. The topography is prairie-like; in this region where the skyscape is dominant, billowing clouds cast moving shadows over patchwork fields. The farms are long and narrow, each with water access to the river, which was the earliest highway. Each village seems cut to a similar pattern: houses with wide verandas and "ski-jump" roofs, a municipal wharf, and

a magnificent Roman Catholic church with silver steeple. One such typically French village is Lefaivre, a preferred destination among photographers who are attracted by the distinctive ambience.

Follow the river road (County Road 24) through Lefaivre to L'Orignal, perhaps the oldest settlement in the lower Ottawa Valley and once part of the only seigneury established in Ontario (1674). You won't overlook the courthouse, which is a remarkable stone building with a blazing red roof. This is the oldest courthouse in Ontario, built in the neoclassical style in 1825. Right beside the courthouse is a United Church that is one of the oldest in Ontario still in use: it was constructed in 1836 as a Church of Scotland. La Bonne Bouche Bakery on the main street is well known for its excellent éclairs and other pastries.

Retrace your tracks upriver to Lefaivre. Follow signs or topography down to the river bank and board the ferry for a brief cruise to the province of Quebec. From the car it is difficult to see the ferry deck, so you seem to be floating on the water itself—an optical illusion that particularly delights kids.

On terra firma again, drive north from the ferry dock through the village of Montebello to the climax of the day—Château Montebello. (Watch carefully for the signs, since the Château itself is hidden behind a dense evergreen forest.)

There are not enough superlatives to describe this perfect resort hotel. First, there is the tremendous building itself, a star-shaped structure of 10,000 red-cedar logs built by 3,500 French-Canadian and Scandinavian craftsmen. The magnificent lobby leaves tourists with their mouths agape: seven storeys of gleaming logs, and in the centre, an appropriately rugged fieldstone fireplace, also seven-storeys high. The construction was front-page news across Canada during the

Cumberland Township Heritage Museum

early 1930s because of the unusual location, lavish design and quick construction (a miraculous four months). Originally used as an exclusive hunting retreat, it is now in the very capable hands of Canadian Pacific.

Second, there is the fabulous property—over 1000 acres of wilderness. The Laurentian Mountains, steep and forested, provide for skiing, fishing and hunting. Alongside the river are golf courses, indoor and outdoor pools, racket courts, a marina (fishing, motor boating, sailing and canoeing), stable, bicycle paths and skating and curling rinks. The grounds include the Papineau Manor, home to Louis-Joseph Papineau (the major political leader in Quebec during the early 1800s), a sumptuously furnished 1850 mansion. Guided tours are provided of this fairy-tale perfect mansion and they are not to be missed, both for the magic of this home and also for a good lesson in Canadian history.

Third, there is the food, wonderful food. Three ample meals a day of continental cuisine exquisitely prepared and served with grace (reservations required). The dining room is a good spot to celebrity-watch, since Montebello is a favoured spot for top-level meetings. International bankers and NATO generals can't all be wrong: Montebello is the Canadian meeting place.

It is very difficult to pull yourself away from Château Montebello—an intoxicating mix of backwoods beauty and sophisticated hospitality—but you can leave knowing that you have had a brief foretaste of heaven.

Cumberland Township Museum
May-September:
Tuesday 1:00-5:00
Wednesday-Friday 10:00-5:00
Saturday & Sunday 11:00-5:00
September to mid-October:
Monday-Friday 1:00-5:00
(613) 833-3059

Château Montebello
(819) 423-6341

BIBLIOGRAPHY

Information on tourist attractions came from many sources. Government publications and brochures printed by public and private facilities are too numerous to mention, but the following published sources deserve recognition.

Angus, Margaret. *The Old Stones of Kingston*. Toronto: University of Toronto Press, 1966.

Bodzin, Gene. *Not Just Another Tour Book. A Practical Guide to the Sights and Traditions of Ottawa*. Ottawa: Footprints of Heritage, 1987.

Bowering, Ian, editor. *Bowering's Guide to Eastern Ontario*. Kingston: Quarry Press, 1992.

Brown, Ron. *Backroads of Ontario*. Edmonton: Hurtig, 1984.

Brown, Ron. *Ghost Towns of Ontario, A Field Guide*. Cannonbooks: Toronto, 1990.

Brown, Ron. *Ghost Towns of Ontario, Volume One*. Cannonbooks: Toronto, 1992.

Chandler, Margaret Ross. *The Great Little Country Inns of Southern Ontario*. Toronto: Deneau, 1989.

Hardy, Anne, editor. *Where to Eat in Canada*. Ottawa: Oberon, 1988.

Kalman, Harold and John Roaf. *Exploring Ottawa: an architectural guide to the nation's capital*. University of Toronto Press: Toronto, 1963.

Mika, Nick and Helma. *Belleville, the Seat of Hastings County*. Belleville: Mika Publishing Company, 1986.

National Capital Commission. *Sculpture Walks. Visual Arts Programme, National Capital Commission*: Ottawa, 1985.

Perkins, Mary Ellen. *Discover Your Heritage, A Guide to Provincial Plaques in Ontario*. Ontario Heritage Foundation: Toronto, 1989.

Preston, Marg. *Capital Kids, Enjoyable Activities In & Around Ottawa*. BG Consultants: Ottawa, 1989.

Teasdale, Shirley. *Hiking Ontario's Heartland*. Whitecap Books: Vancouver, 1993.

This book belongs to

_____

Whatever Next!

First published 1980 by Macmillan Children's Books
This edition published 2011 by Macmillan Children's Books
a division of Macmillan Publishers Limited
20 New Wharf Road, London N1 9RR
Basingstoke and Oxford
Associated companies throughout the world
www.panmacmillan.com

ISBN: 978-1-4472-0262-2

3 5 7 9 8 6 4 2

A CIP catalogue record is available for this book from the British Library.

Printed in China

Whatever Next!

JILL MURPHY

MACMILLAN CHILDREN'S BOOKS

"Can I go to the moon?" asked Baby Bear.

"No, you can't," said Mrs Bear.
"It's bathtime. Anyway, you'd have
to find a rocket first."

Baby Bear found a rocket
in the cupboard under the stairs.

He found a space helmet
on the draining board in the kitchen,
and a pair of space boots
on the mat by the front door.

He packed his teddy
and some food for the journey
and took off up the chimney . . .

. . . WHOOSH! out into the night.

An owl flew past.

"That's a smart rocket," he said.

"Where are you off to?"

"The moon," said Baby Bear.

"Would you like to come too?"

"Yes please," said the owl.

An aeroplane roared out of the clouds.
Baby Bear waved and some of
the passengers waved back.

On and on they flew,
up and up, above the clouds,
past millions of stars till
at last they landed on the moon.

"There's nobody here," said Baby Bear.

"There are no trees," said the owl.

"It's a bit boring," said Baby Bear.

"Shall we have a picnic?"

"What a good idea," said the owl.

"We'd better go," said Baby Bear.
"My bath must be ready by now."
Off they went, down and down.
The owl got out and flew away.
"Goodbye," he said. "It was so nice
to meet you."

It rained and
the rain dripped through
Baby Bear's helmet.

Home went Baby Bear.
Back down the chimney
and on to the living room carpet
with a BUMP!

Mrs Bear came into the room.

"Look at the *state* of you!" she gasped
as she led him away to the bathroom.

"Why, you look as if you've been up the chimney."

"As a matter of fact," said Baby Bear,
"I *have* been up the chimney.
I found a rocket and went to
visit the moon."
Mrs Bear laughed.
"You and your stories," she said.
"Whatever next?"